THE WIT & WISDOM OF
GARDENING

Published in 2012 by Prion
an imprint of the Carlton Publishing Group
20 Mortimer Street
London W1T 3JW

Text compilation copyright © 2012 Nick Holt
Design and layout © 2012 Carlton Books Ltd

ISBN: 978-1-85375-865-2

Printed in China

THE WIT & WISDOM OF
GARDENING

**More than 800 amusing, enlightening
and evergreen quotations**

PRION

How fair is a garden amid the trials and passions of existence.

Benjamin Disraeli

Contents

To the Essex Street crowd,
for their patience

Garden: One of a vast number of free outdoor restaurants operated by charity-minded amateurs in an effort to provide healthful, balanced meals for insects, birds and animals.

Beard & McKie: Gardener's Dictionary •1

And the Lord God planted a garden eastward in Eden.

From the book of Genesis in the Bible •2

It is telling that paradise was an earthly word before a heavenly one. Every garden since has been an oxymoron: little prisons that both venerate the spiritual nature of creation and tacitly slap God on the wrist for making such a chaotic mess of it when he had it to himself.

A.A. Gill •3

The main purpose of a garden is to give its owner the best and highest kind of earthly pleasure.

Gertrude Jekyll No two gardens are the same •4

No two days are the same in one garden.

Hugh Johnson •5

Gardening does give one back a sense of proportion about everything — except itself.

May Sarton Plant Dreaming Deep •6

The trouble with gardening is that it does not remain an avocation. It becomes an obsession.

Phyllis McGinley, The Province of the Heart •7

First, come spring and summer but then we have fall and winter. And then we get spring and summer again. *Peter Sellers as Chauncey, the simpleton gardener mistaken for a guru in Being There •8*

A garden is never so good as it will be next year. *Thomas Cooper •9*

Organic gardening is a different approach rather than a set of methods that can just be substituted for the artificial regime of sprays and fertilisers.
Bob Flowerdew •10

A garden is not made in a year; indeed it is never made in the sense of finality. It grows, and with the labour of love should go on growing.
Frederick Eden A Garden in Venice •11

Gardening is an exercise in optimism. Sometimes, it is the triumph of hope over experience. *Marina Schinz* •12

Let no one think that real gardening is a bucolic and meditative occupation. It is an insatiable passion, like everything else to which a man gives his heart. *Karel Capek* •13

Success, they say, is a matter of being in the right place at the right time. Perhaps more than is the case in life, in the garden you can often alter the place (and indeed sometimes even the time). *Michael Pollan*, Second Nature •14

The unmulched garden looks to me like some naked thing which for one reason or another would be better off with a few clothes on. *Ruth Stout* •15

For most of us who are intimidated by theories of garden design, the cottage garden provides immediate appeal, since it is a horticultural rather than an architectural solution to a limited area. *Patricia Thorpe* •16

The garden is growth and change and that means loss as well as constant new treasures to make up for a few disasters. *May Sarton* •17

Wherever humans garden magnificently,
there are magnificent heartbreaks.
Henry Mitchell, **The Essential Earthman** •18

A killing frost devastates the heart as well as the garden.
Eleanor Perenyi, **Green Thoughts** •19

The garden that is finished is dead.

H.E. Bates **author of The Darling Buds of May** •20

We had better find a way to grow
things in asphalt before we cover
the world with it. *Roger B. Swain,* **Groundwork: A Gardener's Ecology** •21

14

We were misled into believing that pesticides and weedkillers were essential to farm and garden practice, and this resulted in a vast industry, with unsustainable reliance on petrochemicals that polluted our water, destroyed wildlife and wildflowers, and produced food and soil short of essential nutrients and contaminated with residues.

Bob Flowerdew pulls no punches •22

A garden is like those pernicious machineries which catch a man's coat-skirt or his hand, and draw in his arm, his leg, and his whole body to irresistible destruction.

Ralph Waldo Emerson •23

As long as the roots are not severed, all is well, and all will be well, in the garden.
Peter Sellers as Chauncey in **Being There** •24

Most civilised people prefer the shade of some dear family tree to the opulence of a parterre, displaying its patter under the wide open sky.

Harold Nicholson •25

The size of a garden has very little to do with its merit. It is the size of the owner's heart and brain and goodwill that will make his garden either delightful or dull. *Gertrude Jekyll* •26

It isn't that I don't like sweet disorder, but it has to be judiciously arranged.
Vita Sackville West •27

Gardening is a kind of disease. It infects you, you cannot escape it. When you go visiting, your eyes rove about the garden; you interrupt serious cocktail drinking because of an irresistible impulse to get up and pull a weed.

Lewis Gannit •28

One of the most delightful things about a garden is the anticipation it provides.

W. E. Johns •29

It is always exciting to open the door and go out into the garden for the first time on any day.

Marion Cran •30

Sitting in your garden is a feat to be worked at with unflagging determination and single-mindedness... I am deeply committed to sitting in the garden. *Mirabel Osler* •31

I suppose for most people one of the darker joys of gardening is that once you've got started it's not at all hard to find someone who knows a little bit less than you. *Allen Lacy,* **Home Ground** •32

If gardening isn't a pleasure for you, chances are the work will merely give you a rotten disposition. If you'd rather be golfing or fishing, get a bumper sticker that says so, and forget gardening. ***Elsa Bakalar,* A Garden of One's Own** •33

I have never had so many good ideas day after day as when I work in the garden.

John Erskine, US educator, musician and novelist •34

Next time you're thinking of going to the cinema and splurging £30, why not just pop off to the garden centre, get trowels, compost and a few plants and have a lovely afternoon outside?

Kim Wilde, celebrity gardener, on encouraging children to garden, Sunday Times •35

The love of gardening is a seed once sown that never dies.

Gertrude Jekyll •36

Horticulture… is more like falling in love, something that escapes all logic. There is a moment before one becomes a gardener, and a moment after — with a whole lifetime to keep on becoming a gardener.

Allen Lacy, The Inviting Garden •37

Gardening, I told myself, is the most sociable of hobbies. The very nature of one's field of activities demands an audience. No one wants flowers to blush unseen or waste their sweetness.

Barbara Cheney •38

19

What continues to astonish me about a garden is that you can walk past it in a hurry, see something wrong, stop to set it right, and emerge an hour or two later breathless, contented, and wondering what on earth happened. *Dorothy Gilman* •39

My liking for gardens to be lavish is an inherent part of my garden philosophy. I like generosity wherever I find it, whether in gardens or elsewhere. I hate to see things scrimp and scrubby. Even the smallest garden can be prodigal within its limitations.
Vita Sackville West •40

There is now a mobile phone in our pocket or handbag, and a personal computer on the desk… to get away from all this change it is comforting to be able to look over the neighbour's fence and see that at least the world of garden flowers has stayed the same. *Dr D.G. Hessayon from the introduction to*
The New Flower Expert •41

It is utterly forbidden to be half-hearted about gardening. You have got to love your garden whether you like it or not.

W.C. Sellar and R.J. Yeatman Garden Rubbish •42

One of the healthiest ways to gamble is with a spade and a packet of garden seeds. *Dan Bennett* •43

Tomatoes and squash never fail to reach maturity. You can spray them with acid , beat them with sticks and burn them; they love it. *S.J.Perelmann* •44

There's one good thing about snow, it makes your lawn look as nice as your neighbour's. *Clyde Moore* •45

Weather means more when you have a garden. There's nothing like listening to a shower and thinking how it is soaking in around your green beans. *Marcelene Cox* •46

Suburbia is where the developer bulldozes out the trees, then names the streets after them.
Bill Vaughan •47

The architectural feature of all Unpleasaunces is the mysterious little Shed, grey outside and black inside, which no one has the courage to explore on account of the peculiar and distressing smell which seems to be its only inhabitant. *W.C. Sellar and R.J. Yeatman,* Garden Rubbish •48

A garden has a curious, innocent way of consuming cash, while all the time you are under the illusion that you are spending nothing.
Esther Meynell A Woman Talking •49

Long experience has taught me that whereas people will take advice about love, and about money, and about nearly all the problems which beset us in life, they will scarcely ever take advice about their gardens. Well… it may not really matter much, so long as they love them. *Beverley Nichols,* Garden Open Tomorrow •50

While trees are excellent for apes, owls and arboreal fauna in general, they are annoying in a small garden where one hopes to grow something besides a compost pile and a continental championship collection of slugs and sowbugs. *Henry Mitchell* •51

The gardener's autumn begins in March, with the first faded snowdrop.

Karel Capek, The Gardener's Year •52

Of course, at a distant, fleeting glance, you will not see any more of a gardener than his rear end; everything else, like his head, arms and legs, is simply beneath him. *Karel Capek,* The Gardener's Year •53

I find that a real gardener is not a man who cultivates flowers; he is a man who cultivates the soil. *Karel Capek* •54

Crouchers move through a garden at a stoop: naming, gasping, hooraying, admiring or coveting plants; Gapers saunter, smiling or sighing at what they find, succumbing to an intangible beatitude that takes them for a brief escape into another dimension. *Mirabel Osler* •55

In successive censuses gardeners are continuously found at the head of the tables of longevity.

William Beach Thomas, Gardens •56

The most noteworthy thing about gardeners is that they are always optimistic, always enterprising and never satisfied.

Vita Sackville West •57

To enjoy your garden thoroughly, you must say, with Queen Elizabeth, I will have but one mistress here and no master. *from magazine* The Cottage Garden, 1849 •58

My garden is an honest place. Every tree and every vine are incapable of concealment, and tell after two or three months exactly what sort of treatment they have had. *Ralph Waldo Emerson,* Journals •59

One of my pet hates is hearing people refer loftily to real gardeners as a mark of approval, as though there was such a thing as an unreal gardener… It is a completely egalitarian activity. Gardeners are people who garden.

Montagu Don, The Sensuous Garden •60

No class of folk is more keenly aware of how shaky the world is.

Henry Mitchell on Gardening •61

A Gardener's life
Is full of sweets and sours;
He gets the sunshine
When he needs the showers

Reginald Arkell •62

26

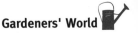

If only one were as good a gardener
in practice as one is in theory, what
a garden one would create!

Vita Sackville West, Some Flowers •63

A good garden cannot be made by
somebody who has not developed the
capacity to know and to love growing things.

Russell Page, The Education of a Gardener •64

Gardeners are — let's face it — control
freaks... The more one thinks about it,
the odder it seems; this compulsion to
remake a little corner of the planet
according to some plan or vision.

Abby Adams, What is a Garden Anyway? •65

I don't dislike gardeners but I'd be just as pleased
with them if they didn't go around trying to make
me feel as if I hated nature. I don't hate it. I just don't
like to grovel in the dirt. *Andy Rooney* •66

The life so short, the craft so long to learn.
This was said about literature, but really
it fits gardening better. Poetry, after all,
is learned extremely early, as a rule, if
it is learned at all, but gardening is the
province of old crocks past the age of 28.
Henry Mitchell, One Man's Garden •67

Any art is long, and the gardening
art is one of the longest.

Leonard H. Robbins, Cure It with a Garden •68

Gardening is a craft, a science, and an art.
To practice it well requires the enthusiasms
of the true amateur and the understanding
of the true student. *Louise and James Bush-Brown* •69

The world is moving into a phase when
landscape design may well be recognized as
the most comprehensive of the arts. Man creates
around him an environment that is a projection
into nature of his abstract ideas. It is only in the present
century that the collective landscape has emerged as
a social necessity. We are promoting a landscape art
on a scale never conceived of in history. *Geoffrey Jellicoe* •70

Gardens are the result of a collaboration between art and nature. *Penelope Hobhouse* •71

Like a great poet, Nature knows how to produce the greatest effects with the most limited means.
Heinrich Heine •72

The gardener, with all his assiduity, does not raise such a variety, nor so many successive crops on the same place, as Nature in the very roadside ditches.
Henry David Thoreau •73

Nature writes, gardeners edit.
Roger B. Swain, Groundwork: A Gardener's Ecology •74

Nature soon takes over if the gardener is absent.

Penelope Hobhouse •75

The garden is merely a boundary between us and the wild, a tamed sphere that always wants to revert to wildness. It is sexy and fecund, prone to chaos and pests, bur controlled (we hope) into beauty and order.

Jenny Uglow, **A Little History of British Gardening** •76

Lovers of nature are curiously reluctant to admit that a completely natural garden is a contradiction in terms. *Anne Scott-James,* **The Pleasure Garden** •77

Nature is the gardener's opponent. The gardener who pretends he is in love with her, has to destroy her climaxes of vegetation and make… an alliance with her which she will be first to break without warning, in the most treasonable way she can. She sneaks in, she inserts her weeds, her couch-grass, her ground elder, her plantain, her greenfly and her slugs behind his back. The bitch. *Geoffrey Grigson*, Gardenage •78

The order of things should be somewhat reversed; the seventh day should be man's day of toil and the other six his sabbath of the affections and the soul — in which to range this widespread garden and to drink in the soft influences and sublime revelations of nature.

Henry David Thoreau •79

As I write this, on June 29th, it's time for another storm to smash the garden to pieces, though it may hold off until the phlox, tomatoes, daylilies and zinnias are in full sway. *Henry Mitchell* •80

To every thing there is a season… a time to plant, and a time to pluck up that which is planted

Bible, Ecclesiastes 3:1-2 •81

Our attitude towards plants is a singularly narrow one. If we see any immediate utility in a plant we foster it. If for any reason we find its presence undesirable or merely a matter of indifference, we may condemn it to destruction forthwith. *Rachel Carson* •82

The secret of improved plant breeding, apart from scientific knowledge, is love. *Luther Burbank, American plant breeder and botanist* •83

Though I do not believe that a plant will spring up where no seed has been, I have great faith in a seed. Convince me that you have a seed there, and I am prepared to expect wonders.

Henry David Thoreau, quoted in Faith In A Seed •84

There are two seasonal diversions that can ease the bite of any winter. One is the January thaw. The other is the seed catalogues.

Hal Borland, The New York Times •85

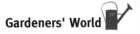
I love being asked to identify plants, and I don't know which gives me more pleasure: to know what they are or not to know what they are. *Elizabeth Lawrence,* **Through the Garden Gates** •86

Plants, like people, are social or anti-social: the good plant has to be able to live amicably with other plants in the border. *Richardson Wright,* **Greedy Gardeners** •87

Any healthy plant will develop shocking bad manners if left to itself. *Fletcher Steele, landscape architect* •88

They know, they just know where to grow, how to dupe you, and how to camouflage themselves among the perfectly respectable plants. They just know, and therefore, I've concluded, weeds must have brains.

Dianne Benson, Dirt •89

A weed is a plant that has mastered every survival skill except for learning how to grow in rows.

Doug Larson, American cartoonist •90

We can in fact only define a weed, mutatis mutandis, in terms of the well-known definition of dirt – as matter out of place. What we call a weed is in fact merely a plant growing where we do not want it. *E.J. Salisbury,* **The Living Garden** •91

I sympathise with weeds perhaps more than the crop they choke, they express so much vigour. They are the truer crop which the earth more willingly bears. *Henry David Thoreau* •92

A weed is no more than a flower in disguise,
Which is seen through at once,
if love give a man eyes.
James Russell Lowell •93

Flowers are for wrapping in cellophane to present as a bouquet;
Flowers are for prize arrangements in vases and silver tea-pots;
Flowers are for plaiting into funeral wreaths;
You can keep your flowers.
Give me weeds.

Norman Nicholson •94

What is a weed? A plant whose virtues have not yet been discovered.

Ralph Waldo Emerson, **Fortune of the Republic** •95

You fight dandelions all weekend, and late Monday afternoon there they are, pert as all get out, in full and gorgeous bloom, pretty as can be, thriving as only dandelions can in the face of adversity. *Hal Borland* •96

Bugs are not going to inherit the earth. They own it now. So we might as well make peace with the landlord.

Thomas Eisner •97

There is no The End to
be written, neither can
you, like an architect,
engrave in stone the day
the garden was finished;
a painter can frame his
picture, a composer notate
his coda, but a garden is
always on the move.

Mirabel Osler •98

Don't underestimate the therapeutic value of
gardening. It's the one area where we can all
use our nascent creative talents to make a truly
satisfying work of art. Every individual, with
thought, patience and a large portion of help from
nature, has it in them to create their own private
paradise: truly a thing of beauty and a joy for ever.

Geoff Hamilton, Paradise Gardens •99

Everything that slows us down and forces
patience, everything that sets us back into
the slow circles of nature, is a help.
Gardening is an instrument of grace.

May Sarton •100

Just a few minutes of quiet relaxation
amongst trees, with bird song and bumblebees
for entertainment, and even the most exhausted
of city workers is ready for anything.

Chris Baines How to Make a Wildlife Garden •101

So long as I can get home and do some digging in my
garden, I'm all right. Marvellous therapy, gardening.

Peggy Lee, American singer, quoted in New York World Telegram •102

44

A gardener is never shut out from his garden,
wherever he may be. Its comfort never fails. Though
the city may close about him, and the grime and the
soot descend upon him, he can still wander in his
garden, does he but close his eyes. *Beverley Nichols* •103

As I have gardened, feeling myself
in some sort of deep dialogue with
an unseen and silent partner, I have
come to know true inner peace.
Martha Smith Beds I Have Known •104

A garden is the best alternative therapy.
Germaine Greer •105

Anyone who seeks that 'peace which passeth all understanding'
or, as Buddhists call it, Nirvana, might well turn to his garden
to distract his mind from the daily anxieties of life.
Frank Kingdon Ward, The Romance of Gardening •106

If you would have a lovely garden, you should live a lovely life. *Shaker proverb* •107

My spirit was lifted and my soul nourished by my time in the garden. It gave me a calm connection with all of life, and an awareness that remains with me now, long after leaving the garden.

Nancy Ross •108

There is a continuity about the garden and an order of succession in the garden year which is deeply pleasing.
Susan Hill •109

From land to land; and in my breast
Spring wakens too; and my regret
Becomes an April violet,
And buds and blossoms like the rest.

Alfred Lord Tennyson, **In Memoriam, XI** •110

The whole essence of joy, if one loves the garden, is to struggle to the ideal beauty in one's own pig-headed way.

Marion Cran, The Garden of Ignorance •111

When I have trouble writing, I step outside my studio into the garden and pull weeds until my mind clears — I find weeding the best therapy there is for writer's block.

Irving Stone •112

All my hurts
My garden spade can heal

Ralph Waldo Emerson, Musketaquid •113

Flowers seem intended for the solace of ordinary humanity. *John Ruskin* •114

The greatest gift of the garden is
the restoration of the five senses.

Hanna Rion, Let's Make a Flower Garden •115

A garden is to be enjoyed and should satisfy the mind and not only the eye of the beholder.

Penelope Hobhouse •116

My good hoe as it bites the ground revenges my wrongs,
and I have less lust to bite my enemies. In smoothing the
rough hillocks, I smooth my temper. *Ralph Waldo Emerson* •117

A perfect summer day is when the sun is shining,
the breeze is blowing, the birds are singing,
and the lawn mower is broken.

James Dent •118

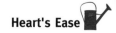

Gardening is a very calming, non-threatening type of activity. Plants don't discriminate. They don't care if a person is twenty-five or eighty-five, in a wheelchair or standing.

Joel Flagler, The New York Times •119

It is good to be alone in a garden at dawn or dark so that all its shy presences may haunt you and possess you in a reverie of suspended thought. *James Douglas,* Down Shoe Lane •120

Gardening is great for helping with P.M.T.
Kim Wilde •121

To be overcome by the fragrance of flowers is a delectable form of defeat.

Beverley Nichols •122

49

"...the one smell that is
beautiful than the
impossible to capture
garden, is the smell of
immediately after a

more heartracingly
scent of any plant and
or contain within a
warm, dusty soil
ight shower of rain. **"**

Montagu Don, The Sensuous Garden •123

Keep a green tree in your heart and perhaps the singing bird will come.

Chinese proverb •124

A woodland in fall color is awesome as forest fire, in magnitude at least, but a single tree is like a dancing tongue of flame to warm the heart. *Hal Borland,* **Sundial of the Seasons** •125

Why are there trees I never walk under but large and melodious thoughts descend upon me?
Walt Whitman, **Song of the Open Road** •126

How I would love to be transported into a scented Elizabethan garden with herbs and honeysuckles, a knot garden and roses clambering over a simple arbor...

Rosemary Verey •127

While it is not obligatory to dabble your bare feet in the dirt to get the most out of your garden, it is a pity not to go barefoot at some time.

Montagu Don, The Sensuous Garden •128

In my garden there is a large place for sentiment. My garden of flowers is also my garden of thoughts and dreams. The thoughts grow as freely as the flowers, and the dreams are as beautiful. *Abram L. Urban* •129

How fair is a garden amid the trials and passions of existence.

Benjamin Disraeli •130

Flowers always make people better,
happier, and more helpful; they are
sunshine, food and medicine to the soul.

Luther Burbank, American plant breeder and botanist •131

Into your garden you can walk
And with each plant and flower talk;
View all their glories, from each one
Raise some rare meditation.
Recount their natures, tell which are
Vertuous like you, as well as fair.

John Rea, Flora, Ceres and Pomona •132

You must not know too much, or be too precise or scientific
about birds and trees and flowers and watercraft; a certain
free margin, and even vagueness, …perhaps ignorance,
credulity, — helps your enjoyment of these things.

Walt Whitman •133

The first gatherings of the garden in May of salads,
radishes and herbs made me feel like a mother
about her baby — how could anything so beautiful
be mine. And this emotion of wonder filled me for
each vegetable as it was gathered every year. There is
nothing that is comparable to it, as satisfactory or as
thrilling, as gathering the vegetables one has grown.

Alice B Toklas •134

Usually, children spend more time in the garden
than anybody else. It is where they learn about the
world, because they can be in it unsupervised,
yet protected. Some gardeners will remember
from their own earliest recollections that no
one sees the garden as vividly, or cares about it
as passionately, as the child who grows up in it.

Carol Williams, **Bringing a Garden to Life** •135

I know nothing so pleasant as to sit there on a summer afternoon, with the western sun flickering through the great elder-tree, and lighting up our gay parterres, where flowers and flowering shrubs are set as thick as grass in a field, a wilderness of blossom, interwoven, intertwined, wreathy, garlandy, profuse beyond all profusion. *Mary Mitford,* Our Village •136

This was among my prayers: a piece of land not so very large, where a garden should be and a spring ever-flowing.

Horace, Satires •137

Not every soil can bear all things.

Virgil, Georgic II •138

The monks were fond of horticulture. Its gentle exercise and placid recreation suited their habits. They planted the best fruit-trees, flowers, and herbs which those ages could furnish.

Owen & Blakeway; **A History of Shrewsbury** •139

What was paradise, but a garden full of vegetables and herbs and pleasure? Nothing there but delights.

William Lawson, maybe the first serious Western garden writer •140

Whan that Aprill with his shoures soote
The droghte of March hath perced to the roote.

Chaucer, Canterbury Tales, Prologue •141

The Lily is an herbe with a white flower:
and though the leaves of the flower be white, yet
within shineth the likeness of golde. The Lily is next
to the Rose in worthines and nobleness.

Bartholomacus Angelicus, De Proprietatibus Rerum, 1492 •142

As for Rosemarie, I lett it runne
all over my garden walls, not onlie
because my bees love it, but because
'tis the herb sacred to remembrance
and, therefore, to friendship.

Sir Thomas More •143

Here remember, that you never take in hand
or begin weeding of your beds, before the
earth be made soft, through the store of rain,
falling a day or two before. *Thomas Hyll* •144

Sowe Carrets in your Gardens, and humbly praise God for them, as for a singular and great blessing.

Richard Gardiner, from Profitable Instructions for the Manuring, Sowing and
Planting of Kitchen Gardens *(1599)* •145

Nothing is more pleasant to the eye
than green grass kept finely shorn.

Francis Bacon, Of Gardens, 1625 •146

As is the garden such is the gardener.
A man's nature runs either to herbs or weeds.

Francis Bacon •147

God Almighty first planted a garden; and, indeed, it is the purest of human pleasures.

Francis Bacon, from Essays (1625) •148

There ought to be gardens for all months in the year, in which, severally, things of beauty may be then in season.

Francis Bacon •149

Love your neighbour, yet pull not downe your hedge.

George Herbert, Welsh poet, Outlandish Proverbs, *1640* •150

A house though otherwise beautifull, yet if it hath no Garden belonging to it, is more like a Prison than a House.

Willam Coles , The Art of Simpling, *1656* •151

Gardens were before gardeners,
and but some hours after the earth.
Sir Thomas Browne, The Garden of Cyrus, *1658* •152

Oh, the incredible profit
by digging of ground!

Thomas Fuller, English churchman and historian, History of the Worthies of England, *1662* •153

A Gard'ner's Work is never at an end; it begins with
the Year, and continues to the next.
John Evelyn, Kalendarium Hortense, *1664* •154

There is not amongst Men
a more laborious Life than
is that of a good Gard'ners.
John Evelyn, Kalendarium Hortense, *1664* •155

In all places where there is a Summer and a Winter, and where your Gardens of pleasure are sometimes clothed with their verdant garments, and bespangled with variety of Flowers, and at other times wholly dismantled of all these; here to recompense the loss of past pleasures, and to buoy up their hopes of another Spring, many have placed in their Gardens, Statues, and Figures of several Animals, and great variety of other curious pieces of Workmanship, that their walks might be pleasant at any time in those places of never dying pleasures. *John Worlidge,* Systema Horticuluturae, *1677* •156

I value my garden more for being full of blackbirds than of cherries, and very frankly give them fruit for their songs.
Joseph Addison •157

Many things grow in the garden that were never sown there.

Thomas Fuller, Gnomologia, *1732* •158

Encouraging his wealthy clients to tear out their splendid formal gardens and replace them with his facile compositions of grass, tree clumps and rather shapeless pools and lakes.

Russell Page on Capability Brown •159

He leaped the fence, and saw that all nature was a garden.

Horace Walpole, On Modern Gardening, *1780,* referring to the landscape designer William Kent •160

Fathers, instill in your children the garden-mania.

Charles Joseph, Prince de Ligne, Coup D'œil sur Belœil, *1781* •161

It must at least be confessed that to embellish the form of nature is an innocent amusement.

Samuel Johnson, on William Shenstone, 'The Lives of the Poets', *1781* •162

There is no virtue which I do not attribute to a
man who loves to project and execute gardening.

Charles Joseph, Prince de Ligne, Coup D'œil sur Belœil, *1781* •163

I never saw daffodils so beautiful. They grew
among the mossy stones about and about them;
some rested their heads upon the stones as on
a pillow for weariness; and the rest tossed and reeled
and danced, and seemed as if they verily laughed
with the wind that blew upon them over the lake.

Dorothy Wordsworth, Grasmere Journal, *1802* •164

We saw the palace and garden of Versailles…
full of statues, vases, fountains, and colonnades.
In all that belongs essentially to a garden they
are extraordinarily deficient.

Percy Bysshe Shelley, Journal, *1816* •165

Nothing is more the child of art than a garden.

Sir Walter Scott •166

If well managed, nothing is more beautiful than the kitchen-garden: the earliest blossoms come there: we shall seek in vain for flowering shrubs… to equal the peaches, nectarines, apricots and plums. *William Cobbett,* **The English Gardener** •167

I have never, for any eight months together, during my whole life, been without a garden.
William Cobbett •168

The form of the orange-tree, the cocoa-nut, the mango, the tree-fern, the banana, will remain clear and separate; but the thousand beauties which unite these into one perfect scene must fade away; yet they will leave, like a tale told in childhood, a picture full of indistinct, but most beautiful figures.
Charles Darwin, **The Voyage of the Beagle,** *1839* •169

A lady, with a small, light spade may, by taking time, succeed in doing all the digging that can be required in a small garden.

Jane Loudon, **Instructions on Gardening for Ladies, 1840** •170

Spinsters… should take up gardening as a Distraction from the unavoidable Disappointments and Trials of Life.

Louisa Johnson, **Every Lady Her Own Flower Gardener** •171

The spirit of some druid seems to animate Mr Paxton in these bulky removals.

The 6th Duke of Devonshire (1844) on Paxton's rock garden at Chatsworth •172

I wish to build my fame upon this structure at Kew, which will be unequalled as yet, by very far and not likely to be surpassed.

RichardTurner, designer of the Palm House at Kew •173

We always feel welcome when, on entering a room, we find a display of flowers on the table. Where there are flowers about, the hostess appears glad, the children pleased, the very dog and cat grateful for our arrival, the whole scene and all the personages seem more hearty, homely and beautiful, because of the bewitching roses, and orchid, and lilies, and mignonette.

Shirley Hibberd, **Rustic Adornments for Homes of Taste,** *1856* •174

Flowers are the sweetest things God ever made and forgot to put a soul into.

Henry Ward Beecher, **Life Thoughts,** *1858* •175

Earth is here so kind, that just tickle her with a hoe and she laughs with a harvest.

Douglas William Jerrold, **A Land of Plenty, (about Australia),** *1859* •176

68

Did you ever meet a gardener, who, however fair
his ground, was absolutely content and pleased?...
Is there not always a tree to be felled or a bed
to be turned?...Is there not ever some grand
mistake to be remedied next summer?

Reverend S. Reynolds Hole, A Book About Roses, *1870* •177

A garden is for comfort, and convenience, and luxury, and use, as well as for making a beautiful picture. It is to express civilisation, and care, and design, and refinement.

Edward Kemp •178

Your spring is passed in anxious doubts and fears, which are usually realized; and so a great moral discipline is worked out for you.

Charles Dudley Warner, **My Summer in a Garden,** *1871* •179

The Amen! of Nature is always a flower.

Oliver Wendell Holmes •180

A garden is a lovesome thing, God wot!

T.E. Brown, **My Garden,** *1893* •181

Last night, there came a frost, which has done great damage to my garden…It is sad that Nature will play such tricks on us poor mortals, inviting us with sunny smiles to confide in her, and then, when we are entirely within her power, striking us to the heart.

Nathaniel Hawthorne, The American Notebooks •182

As to the garden, it seems to me its chief fruit is — blackbirds.

William Morris, Letter to his daughter Jenny, August 24th 1888, The Collected Letters of William Morris, *1987*, ed Norman Kelvin •183

To plow, to plant, to hoe, Is the work which lies before us now.

The Old Farmer's Almanac, *c1882* •184

Nothing is so interesting as weeding.
I went crazy over the outdoor work,
and had at last to confine myself
to the house, or literature must
have gone by the board.

Robert Louis Stevenson, Letter to Sir Sidney Colvin
from Samoa, *1890* •185

It is a golden maxim to cultivate the garden for
the nose, and the eyes will take care of themselves.
Robert Louis Stevenson •186

Never dare tell me again anything about "green grass".
Tell me how the lawn was flecked with shadows. I know
perfectly well that grass is green. So does everybody
else in England… Make me see what it was that made
your garden distinct from a thousand others.
Robert Louis Stevenson •187

From the roofs of the buses they had a fine view
Of the ladies in bloomers who gardened at Kew.
The orchids were slighted, the lilies were scorned,
The dahlias were flouted, till botanists mourned,
But the Londoners shouted, What ho there, Go to;
Who wants to see blooms now you've bloomers at Kew.

Popular poem referring to the special bloomers worn as uniform by the female gardeners at Kew, first employed in 1895. •188

The garden is never dead; growth
is always going on, and growth that
can be seen, and seen with delight.

Canon Ellacombe, from In My Vicarage Garden and Elsewhere •189

Half the interest of a garden is the constant exercise of the imagination.

Mrs C.W. Earle, Pot-Pourri from a Surrey Garden, *1897* •190

If only I could dig and plant myself!...I did one warm Sunday
in last year's April during the servant's dinner hour...slink out
with a spade and a rake and feverishly dig a little piece of ground
and break it up and sow surreptitious ipomaea and run back very
hot and guilty into the house and get into a chair and behind
a book and look languid just in time to save my reputation.

Elizabeth Von Arnim, Elizabeth and Her German Garden, *1898* •191

I am spending delightful afternoons
in my garden, watching everything
living around me. As I grow older,
I feel everything departing, and I
love everything with more passion.

Emile Zola, (in the year of his death, *1902*) •192

To make a great garden, one must have a great idea or a great opportunity.

Sir George Sitwell, Essay on the Making of Gardens, *1909* •193

74

I think the true gardener is a lover of flowers,
not a critic of them. I think the true gardener is
the reverent servant of nature, not her truculent,
wife-beating master. I think the true gardener,
the older he grows, should more and more develop
a humble, grateful and uncertain spirit.
Reginald Farrer, **In a Yorkshire Garden,** *1909* •194

And when your back stops aching
and your hands begin to harden,
You will find yourself a partner
in the glory of the garden.

Rudyard Kipling, **The Glory of the Garden,** *1911* •195

The usual lawn expresses nothing so much a vacancy of mind or an
impious waste of good material; whereas in a garden any man may be
an artist, may experiment with all the subtleties or simplicities of line,
mass, color, and composition, and taste the god-like joys of the creator.
H.G.Dwight, 1912 •196

Years ago, too, women, — always defined as ladies — plied
outdoor tools in semi-shade, afraid of being considered
vulgar or unfeminine; now the spade is recognized as
an honourable implement in female hands.

Mary Hampden, **Every Woman's Flower Garden,** *1915* •197

There is that in the glance of a flower which may at
times control the greatest of creation's braggart lords.
John Muir, **A Thousand-Mile Walk to the Gulf,** *1916* •198

English homes would lose a great part of their
charm without a flower garden, but the hard
times of today and the possibly harder times
we may expect in the near future, urge on us
the importance of giving food a preference.

*William Rowles in 1917; King George V subsequently replaced the
geraniums outside Buckingham Palace with potatoes* •199

I am not a lover of lawns. Rather I would
see daisies in their thousands, ground ivy,
hawkweed, and even hated plantain with tall
stems, and dandelions with splendid flowers
and fairy down, than the too-well-tended lawn.

W. H. Hudson, **The Book of a Naturalist,** *1919* •200

A garden is a public service and having one a public duty. It is a man's contribution to the community. *Richardson Wright, 1922* •201

I have recently heard it advocated as a shortcut to
harmony that all red and scarlet flowers be banished
from the garden. This, I think, would be sad indeed,
for much of warmth and strength, of flash and spirit
would depart with them. *Louise Wilder, 1935* •202

Hitler could bomb their houses, smash their chicken-runs and rabbit-hutches, but he could never kill their enthusiasm for gardening.

Roy Hay, Gardener's Chance, 1946. A book about the gardeners of East End London who continued to 'dig for victory' in 1940, despite the devastation caused by the Blitz •203

SAY IT WITH FLOWERS
Interflora slogan •204

O, bring me flowers when the last,
Last pulse has told its tale;
They'll cheer the scene amid the blast
That turns the features pale.

Thomas P. Moses •205

Flowers changed the face of the planet.
Without them, the world we know — even
man himself — would never have existed.

Loren Eiseley •206

Flowers are simply tarts.
Prostitutes for the bees.

Richard Griffiths as Uncle Monty in Withnail and I •207

Flowers really do intoxicate me.

Vita Sackville West •208

The actual flower is the plant's highest fulfilment, and are not here exclusively for herbaria, county floras and plant geography: they are here first of all for delight. *John Ruskin* •209

There is material enough in a single flower for the ornament of a score of cathedrals.

John Ruskin, **The Stones of Venice,** *1851* •210

What a desolate place would be a world without flowers! It would be a face without a smile, a feast without a welcome

Clara L. Balfour •211

I must own that I would do almost anything, and grow almost anything, for the sake of a fragrance. *Reginald Farrer,* **In a Yorkshire Garden** •212

A house with daffodils in it is a house
lit up, whether or not the sun be shining
outside. Daffodils in a green bowl — and
let it snow if it will. *A.A. Milne* •213

Of all the floral catalogues, the most
exquisitely tantalizing is the daffodil
catalogue. The further you read, the
deeper the gold. *George H. Ellwanger,* The Garden's Story •214

The daffodil is our doorside queen;
She pushes upward the sword already,
To spot with sunshine the early green.
William Cullen Bryant, An Invitation to the Country •215

To watch the upthrust of a daffodil, to see it take form as
a flower-to-be, to see the bud grow and take on the warmth
of colour – there is the very synthesis of spring.

Hal Borland, Hal Borland's Book of Days •216

When Wordworth's heart with pleasure filled at a crowd of golden daffodils, it's a fair bet he didn't see them two weeks later.

Geoff Hamilton, TV Gardener •217

…here the daffodil,
That love child of the Spring, has lingered on
To vex the rose with jealousy.

Oscar Wilde, The Garden of Eros •218

With daffodils mad footnotes for the spring,
And asters purple asterisks for autumn.
Conrad Aitken, **Preludes for Memnon** •219

What is the best-smelling March flower?
Why not ask what's the best cloud? Yet
I am certain it is not the daffodil,
which smells like a stale balloon.
Jim Nollman, **Why We Garden** •220

Dark ages clasp the daisy root.
James Joyce, **Finnegans Wake** •221

If dandelions were hard to grow, they
would be most welcome on any lawn.
Andrew Mason •222

My first hosta was the common variegated kind, 'Undulata'. It is tough as nails, divides easily, grows fast, but it sure is ugly. I don't know why anyone would ever buy another hosta after growing this dog.

Tony Avent, 'Hostas', in My Favorite Plant *by Jamaica Kincaid* •223

An iris likes to sit on the ground the way a duck sits on the water: half in, half out.

Anne Raver, Deep in the Green •224

I will have no more tall bearded irises. The love affair has ended. *Allen Lacy* •225

If I am lukewarm about the dahlia,
I am red hot about the bearded iris.
I like it without qualification, and
would not be without it in the garden.

*Katherine S. White, 'Irises', in My Favorite Plant
by James Kincaid* •226

It always seems to me that the herbaceous peony is the very epitome of June. Larger than any rose, it has something of the cabbage rose's voluminous quality; and when it finally drops from the vase, it sheds its vast petticoats with a bump on the table, all in an intact heap, much as a rose will suddenly fall, making us look up from our book or conversation, to notice for one moment the death of what had still appeared to be a living beauty. *Vita Sackville West* •227

No garden can really be too small to hold a peony.
Had I but four square feet of ground at my disposal,
I would plant a peony in the center and proceed
to worship. *Mrs. Edward Harding,* Peonies in the Little Garden •228

The fattest and most scrumptious of all flowers,
a rare fusion of fluff and majesty, the peony is
now coming into bloom. *Henry Mitchell* •229

Life without phlox is an error!
Karl Forrester •230

Phloxes smell to me like a combination of
pepper and pig–stye, most brooms of dirty,
soapy bath–sponge, hawthorn of fish–shop,
and meadow–sweet of curry powder.
Edward Augustus Bowles, My Garden in the Summer •231

Over the Sedums I will not linger, for I don't like them; over the delightful Sempervivums I dare not linger, for I like them so much.

Reginald Farrer, My Rock–Garden •232

Do you think amethysts can be the souls of good violets?

L.M.Montgomery, Anne of Green Gables •233

Violets smell like burnt sugar cubes that have been dipped in lemon and velvet.

Diane Ackerman, A Natural History of the Senses •234

I would rather see a field of marigolds with its exuberance and vulgarity — so sensual! — than one little precious darling of a plant.

Nancy Goslee Powers, garden designer •235

88

Marigolds are bright and beautiful if, like cousins, you don't have too many of them at once. *Henry Mitchell* •236

Nobody ever said Marigold is a marigold is a marigold.

The American Rose Society •237

Open afresh your round of starry folds
Ye ardent marigolds

John Keats I stood tip-toe upon a little hill •238

Your African marigolds have just about as much freshness as the leather of a new football, without the quality of being easily kicked out of the way.
Christopher Lloyd, The Well–Tempered Garden •239

Been there. Done that. That's the way many of us feel about tulips.

Franziska Reed Huxley, Garden Design *magazine* •240

Clean as a lady
cool as glass
fresh without fragrance
the tulip was

Humber Wolfe •241

Here tulips bloom as they are told;
Unkempt about those hedges blows
An English unofficial rose.

Rupert Brooke, The Old Vicarage, Grantchester •242

I suppose there must be one or two people
in the world who choose not to like tulips,
but such an aberration is scarcely credible.

Anna Pavord, The Tulip •243

The tulip is a courtly quean,
Whom, therefore, I will shun.

Thomas Hood •244

The tulip's petals shine in dew
All beautiful, but none alike.

James Montgomery, On Planting a Tulip Root •245

There is lately a Flower (shal I call it so? in courtesie
I will tearme it so, though it deserve not the appelation)
a Toolip, which hath engrafted the love and affection
of most people unto it; and what is this Toolip? a
well–complexion'd stink, an ill favour wrapt up
in pleasant colours. *Thomas Fuller,* Antheologia, or The Speech of Flowers:
Partly Morall, Partly Misticall, *1660* •246

Tulips are very beautyful flowers, but
have no scent. They adorn a garden wel,
or the house: their roots are like Onyons,
which you must set out in January if there
be no frost; and after they have done bearing,
about Michaelmas take up the roots out of the
ground, which will be double, and keep them
dry on a Box or Paper against the next year.
Thomas Hill, The Gardener's Labyrinth, *1577* •247

In the watery garden, the dahlias are
the stars of the Fall, from bon–bon pink
to blood red, from pastel to velvet, with
just the right lightness at the tips of their
petals but a shameless opulence deep in
their hearts. *Philippe Delerm in Giverny* •248

Looking at my dahlias one summer day,
a friend whose taste runs to the small and
impeccable said sadly, You do like big
conspicuous flowers, don't you? She meant
vulgar, and I am used to that.

Eleanor Perenyi, Green Thoughts •249

The Dahlia's first duty in life is to flaunt and to swagger
and to carry gorgeous blooms well above its leaves, and on no
account to hang its head. *Gertrude Jekyll,* Wood and Garden •250

Everything is handsome about the geranium not excepting its name.

Leigh Hunt •251

O geraniums, and yours, O foxgloves,
springing up amidst the coppice,
that gave my childish cheeks their rosy warmth

Colette, Sido •252

Such geraniums! It does not
become us poor mortals to be
vain — but really, my geraniums!

Mary Russell Mitford •253

94

Is anything more charming in its way than an old–fashioned single hollyhock in its pink or whire, or yellow, or purple flower, and the little pollen powdered tree springing up from the bottom of the corolla! A bee should be buzzing in it, for a bee is never so deliciously pavillioned as in the bell tent of the hollyhock. *Oliver Wendell Holmes,*
The New York Times Magazine •254

Honeysuckle, whose scent represents the soul of the dew.
Maurice Maeterlinck, **Old-fashioned Flowers** •255

Forsythia is pure joy. There is not an ounce not a glimmer of sadness or even knowledge in forsythia. Pure, undiluted, untouched joy.
Anne Morrow Lindbergh, **Bring Me a Unicorn** •256

The spot of the Foxglove is especially strange, because it draws the colour out of the tissue around it, as if it had been stung, and as if the central colour was really an inflamed spot, with paleness round. *John Ruskin,* **The Queen of the Air** •257

Chrysanthemums, which in their art shade
of mauve, and terra–cotta and russet, smell
of moths, camphorball, and drowned sailors.
Sir Osbert Sitwell •258

A morning glory at my window satisfies me more than the metaphysics of books.

Walt Whitman, Song of Myself XXIV •259

Summer set lip to earth's bosom bare,
And left the flushed print in a poppy there.
Francis Thompson, The Poppy •260

We usually think of the Poppy as a coarse flower;
but it is the most transparent and delicate of all the
blossoms of the field… the Poppy is painted glass; it never
glows so brightly as when the sun shines through it.
Wherever it is seen, against the light or with the light,
always it is a flame, and warms the wind like a blown ruby.
John Ruskin, Proserpina •261

The annual Helianthus or Sunflower
towers like a priest raising the monstrance
over the lesser folk in prayer and strives
to resemble the orb which he adores.

Maurice Maeterlinck, Old-fashioned Flowers •262

Ah Sun-flower! weary of time,
Who countest the steps of the Sun:
Seeking after that sweet golden clime
Where the traveller's journey is done.

William Blake, Ah! Sunflower *from*
Songs of Innocence and of Experience •263

I should like to change into a sunflower
most of all. They're so tall and simple.
What flower would you like to be?

Ruth Gordon as Maude in Harold and Maude •264

All the wars of the world, all the Ceasars, have not the staying power of a lily in a cottage border.

Reginald Farrer, The Rainbow Bridge •265

How splendid in the morning is the lily;
with what grace he throws
His supplication to the rose.

James Elroy Flecker •266

Lilies are a high and haughty race, impatient of cultivation and incalculable of temper.

Reginald Farrer, My Rock-Garden •267

Remember that the most beautiful things in the world are the most useless; peacocks and lilies for instance.

John Ruskin •268

So extensive and beautiful is the genus Lilium, so varied in form, color, and periods of blossoming, that, like the daffodil, a garden might be composed of it alone. We readily concede its beauty; the next thing is to manage it.

George H. Ellwanger, **The Garden's Story** •269

The lily was created on the third day, early in the morning when the Almighty was especially full of good ideas.

Michael Jefferson–Brown, **The Lily: For Garden, Patio and Display** •270

We once had a lily here that bore 108 flowers on one stalk: it was photographed, naturally, for all the gardening papers. The bees came from miles and miles, and there were the most disgraceful Bachannalian scenes: bees hardly able to find their way home.

Edith Sitwell •271

When you have but
two pennies left in the world,
buy a loaf of bread with one
and a lily with the other.

Chinese proverb •272

Orchids are more accomplished at the
sensuous side of life than any of us.

Diana Wells, A Florid Affair', Green Prints •273

Orchis, Ophrys, and the others
of this most haughty and noble
race are unapproachable,
intractable plants in cultivation
unless they happen to have
brought themselves there.

Reginald Farrer, My Rock–Garden •274

…many annuals have passed through the hands of demented hybridists and have surfaced in grotesque forms, with monstrous heads or extra limbs and with every drop of natural grace and simplicity drained from them. *Stephen Lacey,* The Startling Jungle: Colour and Scent in the Romantic Garden •275

A rose is a rose is a rose is a rose.

Gertrude Stein, Sacred Emily •276

Fashions in flowers change as regularly as they do in clothes and cars, and nurserymen are quick to dispose of last-year's-model tulips or hyacinths. But roses were, and are, another matter.

Thomas Christopher In Search of Lost Roses •277

God gave us memories that we
might have roses in December.
J.M. Barrie, Courage •278

Won't you come into the garden?
I would like my roses to see you.

Richard Brinsley Sheridan, on being struck by the beauty of his future wife •279

It is the time you have wasted
for your rose that makes your
rose so important. *Antoine de Saint-Exupery,*
The Little Prince •280

The rose is healthy and robust. It's got a pleasant scent and just like me, it's very good in a bed.

Alan Titchmarsh, on a rose named after him at the Chelsea Flower Show 2005 •281

One of the most tragic things I know about human nature is that all of us tend to put off living. We are all dreaming of some magical rose garden over the horizon instead of enjoying the roses that are blooming outside our windows today.

Dale Carnegie •282

There should be beds of roses,
banks of roses, bowers of roses,
hedges of roses, edgings of roses,
baskets of roses, vistas and
alleys of roses.

Samuel Reynolds Hole •283

The roses were coming into full bloom, and their
scent hung in the warm air like a benediction.

Ellis Peters, The Pilgrim of Hate, *one of the* Brother Cadfael Mysteries •284

As for the roses, you could not help feeling they understood that
roses are the only flowers that impress people at garden-parties;
the only flowers that everybody is certain of knowing.

Katherine Mansfield, The Garden Party •285

As sense-bludgeoning as a rose.

Diane Ackerman, A Natural History of the Senses •286

We can complain because rose bushes have thorns, or rejoice because thorn bushes have roses. *Abraham Lincoln (attrib.)* •287

Roses do comfort the heart.

William Langham, **The Garden of Health** •288

There is simply the rose; it is perfect in every moment of its existence.

Ralph Waldo Emerson •289

'I haven't much time to be fond of anything,' says Sergeant Cuff. 'But when I have a moment's fondness to bestow, most times… the roses get it.' *Wilkie Collins,* **The Moonstone** •290

A Rose is sweeter in the bud than full blown.

John Lyly, sixteenth century English dramatist and author •291

Theophrastus… calleth the Rose
the light of the earth, the faire
bushie toppe of the spring, the fire
of love, the lightning of the land.

John Parkinson, Theatrum Botanicum, 1640 •292

Our highest assurance of the goodness of Providence seems to
me to rest in flowers. All other things, our desires, our food,
are really necessary for our existence in the first instance.
But this rose is an extra. Its smell and its colour are an
embellishment of life, not a condition of it.

Sir Arthur Conan Doyle, The Memoirs of
Sherlock Holmes: The Naval Treaty •293

Lyllies and Roses planted together
will both smell the pleasanter.

William Langham, The Garden of Health, 1579 •294

109

You love the roses – so do I. I wish
The sky would rain down roses, as they rain
From off the shaken bush. Why will it not?
Then all the valleys would be pink and white,
And soft to tread on. They would fall as light
As feathers, smelling sweet; and it would be
Like sleeping and yet waking, all at once.

George Eliot, The Spanish Gypsy •295

He who would have beautiful Roses in his garden must have beautiful Roses in his heart.

Reverend S. Reynolds Hole, A Book About Roses •296

I don't know whether nice people tend to grow roses or growing roses makes people nice.

Roland A. Browne •297

A red florist's rose which has saved more marriages than all the guidance counselors of the world put together.

Peter Beales, Twentieth-Century Roses, *on the rose 'Baccara'* •298

I'd rather have roses on my table
than diamonds on my neck.
Emma Goldman •299

❝And the roses — the roses! Rising
sun-dial, wreathing the tree-trunks
climbing up the walls and spreading
falling in cascades — they came alive
fresh leaves, and buds — and buds —
tiny magic until they burst and uncurled
spilling themselves over their brims

112

out of the grass, tangled round the
and hanging from their branches,
over them with long garlands
day by day, hour by hour. Fair,
at first, but swelling and working
into cups of scent delicately
and filling the garden air. **"**

Frances Hodgson Burnett, The Secret Garden •300

A lovely being, scarcely formed or moulded,
A rose with all its sweetest leaves yet folded.

Lord Byron, Don Juan •301

A single flower he sent me, since we met.
all tenderly his messenger he chose;
deep hearted, pure, with scented dew still wet
One perfect rose. *Dorothy Parker,* One Perfect Rose •302

Go, lovely Rose,
Tell her that wastes her Time and me,
That now she knows,
When I resemble her to thee,
How sweet and fair she seems to be.
Edmund Waller, from Poems, 1645 •303

Gather the Rose of love,
whilest yet is time.

Edmund Spencer, The Faerie Queene, Book II •304

The modest Rose puts forth a thorn:
The humble Sheep a threatning horn:
While the Lilly white, shall in Love delight,
Nor a thorn nor a threat stain her beauty bright
William Blake, The Lilly, from Songs of Innocence and of Experience •305

Greenfly, it's difficult to see
Why God, who made the rose, made thee.
A.P. Herbert, from Look Back and Laugh •306

Then I will raise aloft the milk-white Rose,
With whose sweet smell the air shall be perfumed
William Shakespeare, Henry VI Part II – York •307

There will I make thee a bed of roses
With a thousand fragrant posies, A cap of flowers,
and a kirtle Embroider'd all with leaves of myrtle
William Shakespeare, The Passionate Pilgrim XX •308

The red rose whispers of passion,
And the white rose breathes of love;
O, the red rose is a falcon,
And the white rose is a dove
John Boyle O'Reilly, A White Rose •309

The roses fearfully on thorns did stand.

William Shakespeare, Sonnet XCIX •310

Roses have thorns, and silver fountains mud;…
(Clouds and eclipses stain both moon and sun,)…
And loathsome canker lives in sweetest bud

William Shakespeare, Sonnet XXXV •311

Oh, this is the joy of the rose:
That it blows,
And goes.

Willa Cather •312

What a pother have
authors made with Roses!

Nicholas Culpeper, 17th Century
English herbalist •313

The roses had given up their
annual struggle to keep things
cheerful and now hemmed in
Mr Rowse's path with thorns.

Fay Weldon •314

The Rose has but
a Summer reign,
the Daisy never dies.

James Montgomery, The Daisy — *on finding one in*
Bloom on Christmas Day •315

A pale rose is a smell that has no fountain;
that has upside down the same distinction;
elegance is not coloured, the pain is there.

Gertrude Stein, Geography and Plays •316

There is no gathering the rose
without being pricked by the thorns.

Bidapi, *author of the fourteenth century Arabic* 'Fables of Bidapi' •317

Flower lovers have been
complaining for years
that scent has vanished
from the garden. Put
your nose into a modern
rose and sniff; most often,
nothing at all happens.

Abby Adams, The Gardener's Gripe Book •318

Most modern roses are worth less than the soil they are planted in. Screw up brightly coloured rubbish and pin it to dead bushes to obtain the same effect without the problem of aphids.

Josephine Saxton, Gardening Down a Rabbit Hole •319

I was flattered to have a rose named after me
until I read the description in the catalogue:
no good in a bed, but perfect up against a wall.
Eleanor Roosevelt •320

I hate rose gardens. I never know why people have them – they don't have weigela gardens or philadelphus gardens.

Sir Simon Hornby
President of the RHS •321

God the first garden made,
and the first city, Cain.

Abraham Cowley, **The Garden** •322

Gardening, reading about gardening, and writing about gardening are all one; no one can garden alone.

Elizabeth Lawrence, The Little Bulbs •323

Find a street without a flower, and you may be sure that there the English are in exile, still hoping and planning behind the lace curtain and the aspidistra for a time and place that will break into living blossom.

J. B. Priestley, from English Journey •324

122

Give me odorous at sunrise
a garden of beautiful flowers
where I can walk undisturbed.

Walt Whitman, Give Me the Splendid Silent Sun •325

Tarragon, sage, mint, savory, burnet — opening your
pink flowers at noon, to close three hours later — truly
I love you for yourselves — but I shan't fail to call on
you for salads to go with boiled leg of mutton,
to season sauces; I shall exploit you. *Colette,* Places •326

Cicely: When I see a spade,
I call it a spade.
Gwendolen: I am glad to say that I have
never seen a spade. It is obvious that our
social spheres have been widely different.

Oscar Wilde, The Importance of Being Earnest •327

123

Nature does not complete things. She is chaotic. Man must finish, and he does so by making a garden and building a wall.

Robert Frost •328

'We can talk,' said the Tiger-lily, 'when there's anybody worth talking to.'

Lewis Carroll, **Through the Looking Glass** •329

People from a planet without flowers would think we must be mad with joy the whole time to have such things about us.

Iris Murdoch, **A Fairly Honourable Defeat** •330

I am writing in the garden. To write as one should
of a garden one must write not outside it or merely
somewhere near it, but in the garden.

Francis Hodgson Burnett •331

A garden should be in a constant state of
fluid change, expansion, experiment, adventure;
above all it should be an inquisitive, loving, but
self-critical journey on the part of its owner.

H.E. Bates •332

All gardening is landscape-painting.

Alexander Pope, 1734, cited in Joseph Spence, 'Anecdotes' •333

It is a blessed sort of work, and if Eve had had a spade
in Paradise and known what to do with it, we should
not have had all that sad business of the apple.
Elizabeth Von Arnim •334

Gardens… should be like lovely, well-shaped
girls: all curves, secret corners, unexpected
deviations, seductive surprises and then still
more curves. *H.E. Bates,* **A Love of Flowers,** *1971* •335

A man will talk of love out among the lilacs and the roses, who would be stricken dumb by the demure propriety of the four walls of a drawing-room.

Anthony Trollope, **The Small House at Allington** •336

In fine weather the old gentleman is almost constantly in the garden; and when it is too wet to go into it, he will look out of the window at it, by the hour together. He has always something to do there, and you will see him digging, and sweeping, and cutting, and planting, with manifest delight. *Charles Dickens,* Sketches by Boz •337

Nothing grows in our garden, only washing. And babies.

Dylan Thomas •338

127

The fine old place never looked more like a delightful home than at that moment: the great white lilies were in flower; the nasturtiums, their pretty leaves all silvered with dew, were running away over the low stone wall; the very noises around had a heart of peace within them.

George Eliot, Middlemarch •339

I want death to find me planting my cabbages, but caring little for it, and even less about the imperfections of my garden. *Montaigne*, Essais, *1580* •340

Lord Illingworth: The Book of Life begins with a man and a woman in a garden
Mrs Allonby: It ends with *Revelations*

Oscar Wilde, A Woman of No Importance •341

I am not fond of the idea
of my shrubberies being
always approachable.

Jane Austen, Persuasion •342

Colette wrote of vegetables as if they were love
objects and of sex as if it were an especially
delightful department of gardening.

Brigid Brophy •343

You are no ruin, sir; no lightning-struck tree.
You are green and vigorous; plants will grow
about your roots, whether you ask them or not.

Jane on Mr Rochester's blindness in Charlotte Bronte's Jane Eyre •344

Helen: Do you really edit sex manuals?
George: I really, really do, but I have a confession to make. I'm much better at books on gardening.

That's the end of the book.
I wanted to present it simply
without big character arcs
or sensationalizing the story.
I wanted to show flowers as
God's miracles. I wanted to
show that Orlean never saw
the blooming ghost orchid.
It was about disappointment.

Point is, what's so wonderful is that every one
of these flowers has a specific relationship with
the insect that pollinates it. There's a certain orchid
looks exactly like a certain insect so the insect is
drawn to this flower, its double, its soul mate,
and wants nothing more than to make love to it.
And after the insect flies off, spots another soul-mate
flower and makes love to *it*, thus pollinating it.
And neither the flower nor the insect will ever
understand the significance of their lovemaking.
I mean, how could they know that because
of their little dance the world lives?

Chris Cooper as John Laroche in Adaptation •347

Rosemary and lavender, mint and thyme, all manner of
herbs filled the walled garden with aromatic odours.

Ellis Peters, The Leper of Saint Giles, *one of the* Brother Cadfael Mysteries •348

The return to Fernlight Avenue after
three weeks' absence in midsummer
was always to a garden of dizzying
voluptuousness… The lawn would be
a yard high with hay, the trees would
be scraping the windows and would
have unloaded their fruit on the ground…
The roses would have bloomed and fallen,
leaving puddles of pink petals on the
grass, and the lower end of the garden,
where it narrowed into an avenue
between soft fruits, would be
impenetrable, the blackberries
and raspberries having closed
the gap between themselves.

Gerard Woodward, **August** •349

...a charming paradisical mingling of all
that was pleasant to the eye and good for food.
The rich flower-border running along every walk,
with its endless succession of spring flowers,
anemones, auriculas, wall-flowers, sweet-williams,
campanulas, snap-dragons, and tiger-lilies, had
taller beauties such as moss and Provence roses,
varied with espalier apple trees; the crimson of
a carnation was carried on in the lurking crimson
of the neighbouring strawberry beds; you gathered
a moss rose one moment and a bunch of currants
the next; you were in a delicious fluctuation between
the scent of jasmine and the juice of gooseberries.

George Eliot describing an old country garden in
Scenes of Clerical Life •350

The one small garden of a free gardener was all his need and due, not a garden swollen to a realm; his own hands to use, not the hands of others to command.

J.R.R. Tolkein, The Lord of the Rings — of Samwise Gamgee •351

I like to see flowers growing,
but when they are gathered, they
cease to please. I look on them
as things rootless and perishable;
their likeness to life makes me sad.
I never offer flowers to those I love;
I never wish to receive them from
hands dear to me.

Charlotte Bronte, Villette. •352

But when Beryl looked at the bush, it seemed
to her the bush was sad. We are dumb trees,
reaching up in the night, imploring we know
not what, said the sorrowful bush.

Katherine Mansfield, The Garden Party •353

The world would be a far poorer place if gardeners
throughout history had not been inclined to lay
down their trowels from time to time in favour
of a pen, a typewriter, or a word processor.

Charles Elliot, The RHS Treasury of Garden Writing •354

All grew the old-fashioned cottage
garden flowers, pinks and sweet
Williams and love-in-a-mist.

Flora Thompson, Lark Rise to Candleford •355

It would be idle to deny that those gardens
contained flowers in full measure. They were
bright with Achillea, Bigonia Radicans, Campanula,
Digitalis, Euphorbia, Funkia, Gypsophilia, Helianthus,
Iris, Liatris, Monarda, Phlox Drummondii, Salvia,
Thalictrum, Vinca and Yucca. But the devil of it
was that Agnus McAllister [the head gardener]
would have a fit if they were picked.

P.G. Wodehouse, **Blanding's Castle** •356

Her mother has none of the present
snobbish form of gardening, of balancing
and landscaping even a small area. She
planted exactly where her plants would
do best. From this principle there grew
wandering bows and tidy knots of box
edging, gardens within gardens — Russian
dolls in the spaces — spaces skeleton now
but ever containing small treasures, whether
they flowered in spring, summer or winter.

Molly Keane, **Time after Time** •357

She had never seen a place of which nature had done more, or where natural beauty had been so little counteracted by an awkward taste.

Jane Austen, Pride & Prejudice. *Elizabeth's first view of Pemberley, believed to be based on Chatsworth House* •358

I am thinking of the onion again. …Not self-righteous like the proletarian potato, nor a siren like the apple. No show-off like the banana. But a modest, self-effacing vegetable, questioning, introspective, peeling itself away, or merely radiating halos like ripples.

Erica Jong, Fruits & Vegetables •359

I used to visit and revisit it a dozen times a day, and stand in deep contemplation over my vegetable progeny with a love that nobody could share or conceive of who had never taken part in the process of creation. It was one of the most bewitching sights in the world to observe a hill of beans thrusting aside the soil, or rows of early peas just peeping forth sufficiently to trace a line of delicate green.

Nathaniel Hawthorne •360

Cabbage: A vegetable about as large and wise as a man's head.

Ambrose Bierce, The Devil's Dictionary •361

Little flower, but if I could understand,
what you are, root and all in all,
I should know what God and man is.

Alfred, Lord Tennyson •362

It will never rain roses. When we want to
have more roses, we must plant more roses.

George Eliot •363

Society is like a lawn, where
every roughness is smoothed,
every bramble eradicated,
and where the eye is delighted
by the smiling verdure of
a velvet surface. *Washington Irving* •364

If you live in humble and expectant mood with a garden, in the course of time you will come to know it. And if you begin with a bare and muddy acre, unplanted, unshaped, then you can help to mould the character of the garden to yourself.

Susan Hill, Through The Garden Gate •365

Just living is not enough ...
One must have sunshine,
freedom, and a little flower.

Hans Christian Andersen •366

We must cultivate our garden.

Voltaire, Candide •367

'What a pretty flower, I've never seen one like it; there's no one like you, Oriane, for having such marvellous things in your house,' said the Princesse de Parme... I looked and recognised a plant of the sort that I had watched Elstir painting. 'I am so glad that you like them; they are charming, do look at their little purple velvet collars; the only thing against them is – as may happen to people who are very pretty and very nicely dressed — they have a hideous name and a horrid smell. In spite of which I am very fond of them. But what is rather sad is that they are dying.' *Marcel Proust,* Remembrance of Things Past — The Guermantes Way •368

Without trees the future looks grim…
Trees bring us joy, trees bring communities
alive by reminding us of the changing
seasons, the cycle of life and rebirth.

Alan Titchmarsh, for the Woodland Trust 'Tree for All' campaign •369

Trees inspire us, trees are living monuments that remind us of our duty to all living things. Trees make our world more beautiful and give shelter to insects, animals and birds.

Fay Ripley, actress, for the Woodland Trust 'Tree for All' campaign •370

We all need trees, lots of them, to make our communities greener and healthier places to live. Grey is dull and deadens the soul, green is fresh and makes us feel alive.

Joanna Lumley, actress, for the Woodland Trust 'Tree for All' campaign •371

Trees sing and dance, make faces
and give flower bouquets, trying
to be loved. You ever notice that
trees do everything to get attention
we do, except walk?

Alice Walker, The Color Purple •372

He that plants trees loves others besides himself.

Thomas Fuller, Gnomologia, *1732* •373

Except during the nine months before he draws his first breath, no man manages his affairs as well as a tree does.

George Bernard Shaw •374

Much can they praise the trees so straight and high,
The sailing pine, the cedar proud and tall,
The vine-prop elm, the poplar never dry,
The builder oak, sole king of forests all.

Edmund Spenser, **The Faerie Queene** •375

The tree is known by his fruit.

Bible, **Matthew 12:33** •376

You can't be suspicious of a tree, or accuse a bird or a squirrel of subversion or challenge the ideology of a violet. *Hal Borland,* Sundial of the Seasons •377

I have a particular feeling for this particular tree, and here is where the difficulty is. For I am about to kill it.
Barbara Dean, Hunting a Christmas Tree •378

thou shalt not destroy the trees thereof by forcing an axe against them: for thou mayest eat of them, and thou shalt not cut them down.

Deuteronomy 20:19 •379

A stricken tree, a living thing, so beautiful, so dignified, so admirable in its potential longevity, is, next to man, perhaps the most touching of wounded objects.

Edna Ferber, A Kind of Magic •380

I don't know when tree houses for adults went out of fashion — and still less why. I myself would rather have an arboreal retreat than a swimming pool any day.

Eleanor Perenyi •381

A solitary maple on a woodside flames in a single scarlet, recalling nothing so much as the daughter of a noble house dressed for a fancy ball, with the whole family gathered round to admire her before she goes. *Henry James* •382

Of all man's works of art, a cathedral is greatest.
A vast and majestic tree is greater than that.
Henry Ward Beecher, Proverbs from Plymouth Pulpit •383

If trees could talk they would tell the most amazing stories… Plant a tree and dream.

Hilary McKay, for the Woodland Trust 'Tree for All' campaign •384

Good timber does not grow with ease.
The stronger the wind, the stronger the trees.

J Willard Marriott, businessman and founder of hotel chain •385

The evergreen! How beautiful, how welcome,
how wonderful the evergreen!

Jane Austen, Mansfield Park •386

I do not think anything in Nature is more mysterious
or more effective than a big tree…Standing under this
one and looking up with knitted concentration, quite
baffled, I got the impression that it emanated goodness.
It stood there firmly like a noble thought, which if
understood would save the world.

John Stewart Collins, Trees •387

I think that I shall never see
A poem as lovely as a tree

Joyce Kilmer, Trees •388

150

Trees are the best monuments that a man can erect to his own memory. They speak his praises without flattery and they are blessings to children yet unborn.

Lord Orrery to Thomas Carew, 1749 •389

He who plants a tree, plants a hope

Lucy Larcom, Plant a Tree •390

I never before knew the full value of trees.
My house is entirely embosomed in high plane
trees, with good grass below, and under them I
breakfast, dine, write, read and receive my company.

Thomas Jefferson, an enlightened President •391

I thank you for the seeds… Too old to plant trees for
my own gratification, I shall do it for my posterity.

Thomas Jefferson again •392

A tree is a tree –
how many more do
you need to look at?

Ronald Reagan, 1965 — not so enlightened •393

For in the true nature of things,
if we rightly consider, every green
tree is far more glorious than if it
were made of gold and silver.

Martin Luther King •394

Great trees are good for nothing but shade.

George Herbert, Outlandish Proverbs, *1640* •395

…trees are monuments. Once the decisions
have been made, the roots spread out and
compost laid, then you need only to stand
back for sixty years. It has great charm,
that thought for gardens in the mind.

Mirabel Osler, A Gentle Plea for Chaos •396

I think that I shall never see
A billboard lovely as a tree.
Perhaps, unless the billboards fall,
I'll never see a tree at all.

Ogden Nash, Song of the Open Road •397

Trees are the earth's endless effort to speak to the listening heaven.

Rabindranath Tagore, Fireflies •398

The wonder is that we can see these trees and not wonder more

Ralph Waldo Emerson •399

154

Generations pass while some tree stands, and old families last not three oaks.

Sir Thomas Browne, Hydriotaphia, *1658* •400

The tall Oak, towering to the skies,
The fury of the wind defies,
From age to age, in virtue strong,
Inured to stand, and suffer wrong

James Montgomery •401

When the oak is felled the whole forest echoes with its fall, but a hundred acorns are sown in silence by an unnoticed breeze.

Thomas Carlyle •402

A song to the oak, the brave old oak,
Who hath ruled in the greenwood long;
Here's health and renown to his broad green crown,
And his fifty arms so strong.

H.F. Chorley, **A Song to the Oak** •403

The birch,
most shy
and ladylike
of trees.

James Russell Lowell,
An Indian-Summer Reverie •404

Loveliest of trees,
  the cherry now
Is hung with bloom
  along the bough,
And stands about
  the woodland ride
Wearing white
  for Eastertide

A.E. Housman, from A Shropshire Lad •405

Most trees look older than they are, except for yews, which are even older than they look.

Alan Mitchell, dendrologist, quoted in
Thomas Pakenham's Meetings With Remarkable Trees •406

To plant trees is to give body and life to one's dreams of a better world.
Russell Page, **The Education of a Gardener •407**

In the intimate and humanized landscape, trees become the greatest single element linking us visually and emotionally with our surroundings. Other manifestations of Nature — great rocks, deserts, moors, torrents, hurricanes — stir us, fill us with awe, make us afraid or humble, but a tree we understand and can allow to become part of us. It is no wonder that when we first think of a garden, we think of a tree. *Thomas Church,* **Gardens Are for People •408**

Solitary trees, if they grow at all, grow strong.

Winston Churchill, The River War •409

Of all the ugly things, nothing is worse than the variegated conifer, which usually perishes as soon as its variegated parts die, the half dead tree often becoming a bush full of wisps and hay.

William Robinson, The English Flower Garden •410

There is enough misery in the world without thinking of Norway maples.

Henry Mitchell, The Essential Earthman •411

I would rather look upon a tree in all its luxuriance and diffusion of boughs and branches, than when it is cut and trimmed into mathematical figures.

Joseph Addison, The Spectator •412

A timber tree is a merchant adventurer, you shall never know his worth 'til he be dead.

John Evelyn, Sylva •413

It's easy to be cavalier about clearing when 'chain saw fever' strikes, but 'oops' won't replace a tree mistakenly felled in haste. *Ann Lovejoy,* Gardening from Scratch •414

Together with a few human beings, dead and living, and their achievements, trees are what I most love and revere.

Hildegard Flanner •415

The owner of a new garden probably ought to spend his first year with his hands tied behind his back and his tools locked away in the cellar. The savings in plants and time would be remarkable. Gardeners know this, but if not restrained they forget all good sense at the sight of new soil.

Thomas C. Cooper •416

The would-be gardener requires more patience than most mortals! *Celia Thaxter* •417

Gardeners have three weapons to use against summer drought: mulches, watering pots, and prayers.

Tyler Whittle, **Some Ancient Gentlemen** •418

An old way that farmers in the west of England and in parts of America judged whether their soil was ready for sowing in the spring was to go into the field, drop their pants, and sit bare-cheeked on the ground. If the earth felt warm to their buttocks, it was ready.

Montagu Don, The Sensuous Garden •419

Never dig without a reason.
William Bryant Logan, Dig We Might, Garden Design magazine •420

The best way to garden is to put on a wide-brimmed straw hat and some old clothes. And with a hoe in one hand and a cold drink in the other, tell somebody else where to dig.

Tex Bix Bender, **Don't Throw in the Trowel** •421

What a man needs in gardening is a cast-iron back, with a hinge in it.

Charles Dudley Warner,
My Summer in a Garden •422

If a young man with an elementary knowledge of gardening can be found, who wants to learn, is strong, willing and intelligent, it is better to supply most of the brains yourself.

Helena Rutherfurd Ely, **A Woman's Hardy Garden** •423

If there is too much work, reflect on why heaven makes teenage boys. If you stand there and direct the boys, they can do a passable job for a modest amount of money.

Jeff Cox, Creating a Garden for the Senses •424

If you bee not able, nor willing to hyre a gardner, keepe your profites to your selfe, but then you must take all the paines.

William Lawson, A New Orchard and Garden, *1618* •425

A man should never plant a garden larger than his wife can take care of.

T.H. Everett •426

However small your garden, you must provide for two of the serious gardener's necessities; a tool shed and a compost heap.

Anne Scott-James, **Down To Earth** •427

It has always amazed me that manufacturers of slug bait, and other such garden aids, should proudly announce on the label that their product is 'harmless to pets'. A pesticide that could guarantee to cause pets irreparable damage would, I'd have thought, sell like hot cakes.

John Carey, **The Sunday Times** •428

As a keen gardener I am a regular drowner of slugs in beer.

Ben Bradshaw, Junior Environment Minister •429

The true gardener must be brutal – and imaginative for the future.

Vita Sackville West, More for Your Garden •430

To have an environmentally native garden, it is not enough just to sit back and let the weeds grow tall; you must, it turns out, be as aggressive as though you were attempting a Versailles.

Abby Adams, **The Gardener's Gripe Book** •431

I cannot lay too great stress upon the neatness in which a lady's garden should be kept. If it is not beautifully neat, it is nothing.

Marie E. Jackson, **The Florist's Manual** •432

Designing a garden is the beginning of a series of mistakes.

Mirabel Osler, **Garden Design magazine** •433

The secret of landscapes isn't creation…It's maintenance.

Michael Dolan, Garden Design magazine •434

Good pruning is invisible. It looks as if everything grew to the right size and stopped.

Cass Turnbull, quoted in Horticulture magazine •435

There is a psychological distinction between cutting back and pruning. Pruning is supposed to be for the welfare of the tree or shrub; cutting back is for the satisfaction of the cutter.

Christopher Lloyd, The Well-Tempered Garden •436

Remember: no plant needs pruning. We prune for human, not horticultural requirements.

Montagu Don, The Sensuous Garden •437

The best time to take cuttings
is when no one is looking.

Bob Flowerdew •438

Over-fertilized plants may be beautiful but are
otherwise useless, like people whose energies
are devoted so completely to their appearance
that there is no other development.

William Longgood •439

Throw all preconceived notions out of the window, plant
wildly, laugh at failures, and smugly savour the successes.

Dan Hinkley, **The Explorer's Garden: Rare and Unusual Plants** •440

The best advice I ever received about gardening
was to plant the bones early and not to worry
about the details; they could adapt and change as
inclination and experience allowed.

Montagu Don, **The Sensuous Garden** •441

For garden best
Is south south-west
Good tilth brings seedes,
Evil tilture, weedes

Thomas Tusser, **Five Hundred Points**
of Good Husbandrie, *1573* •442

A good gardener always plants three seeds — one for
the grubs, one for the weather, and one for himself.

C. Collins •443

It is said that hanging a scythe in a plum-tree,
or an iron hoop, or horse shoes, will insure a
crop of plums. This ought to be investigated.

Henry Ward Beecher •444

This rule in gardening never forget:
to sow dry and to set wet. **English Proverb** •445

Acid-loving plants are often blue-flowered. Most of them will not survive in limey soil. It is a waste of time and money to try, but you will.

Josephine Saxton, Gardening Down a Rabbit Hole •446

Perennials are the ones that grow like weeds, biannuals are the ones that die this year instead of next and hardy annuals are the ones that never come up at all.

Katherine Whitehorn, Observations •447

Sooner or later one has to make up one's mind as to whether half-hardy annuals are worth growing or not. They certainly take up a lot of time, and once the frost has cut them down they are gone forever, and all our labour with them. *Vita Sackville West,* Some Flowers •448

I consider every plant hardy until I have killed it myself.

Sir Peter Smithers, noted Swiss plantsman •449

"Always try to grow in plant or plants out of your neighbours never can receive no greater a gardener of equal before your plants and

your garden some
the ordinary, something
attempted. For you
flattery than to have
intelligence stand
ask, 'What is that?' "

Richardson Wright, Another Gardener's Bed-Book •450

Sowe carrots in your Gardens, and humbly praise
God for them, as for a singular and great blessing.

Richard Gardiner, **Profitable Instructions for the
Manuring, Sowing and Planting of Kitchen Gardens,** *1599* •451

You may go into the field or down the lane, but don't go into Mr. McGregor's garden.

Beatrix Potter, **The Tale of Peter Rabbit** •452

Don't wear perfume in the garden —
unless you want to be pollinated by bees.

Anne Raver, **Deep in the Green** •453

I will keep returning to the virtues of sharp and swift drainage, whether a plant prefers to be wet or dry…I would have called this book Better Drains, but you would never have bought it or borrowed it for bedtime.

Robin Lane-Fox •454

For my part I cast my nail-parings out of the bathroom window so as to feed the ceanothus below with hoof and horn. Since, at thirty years, this is the oldest ceanothus in my garden, and it is still flourishing, I naturally congratulate myself on a sagacious policy.

Christopher Lloyd •455

Never go to a doctor whose office plants have died. *Erma Bombeck* •456

Hurt not the earth,
neither the sea,
nor the trees.

Revelation, 7:3 •457

Remain true to the earth.

Friedrich Nietzsche, **Thus Spake Zarathustra** •458

And Adam was a gardener.

Cade to Sir Humphrey and Stafford, Henry VI Part II, **IV, ii** •459

There is no ancient gentlemen but gardeners… They hold up Adam's profession. *First Clown,* Hamlet, V, i •460

Our bodies are our garden, to the which
Our will are gardeners.
Iago to Roderigo, Othello, I, iii •461

Rough winds do shake the darling buds of May

Sonnet XVIII •462

God saw him when he was hid in the garden.

Claudio to Don Pedro, of Benedick, Much Ado about Nothing, **V, i** •463

This goodly frame, the earth, seems to me a sterile promontory

Hamlet to Rosencrantz and Guildenstern, Hamlet II, ii •464

Who plucks the bud before one leaf put forth?
If springing things be any jot diminish'd,
They wither in their prime, prove nothing worth

Venus and Adonis •465

Things growing to themselves are growth's abuse:
Seeds spring from seeds and beauty breedeth beauty

Venus and Adonis •466

Now 'tis the spring, and weeds are shallow-rooted;
Suffer them now, and they'll o'ergrow the garden
And choke the herbs for want of husbandry

Queen Margaret, Henry VI, Part II, **Act III, i** •467

Fie on't! O fie! 'tis an unweeded garden,
That grows to seed; things rank and gross in nature
Possess it merely *Hamlet's soliloquy,* Hamlet, **I, ii** •468

Under the cool shade of a sycamore
I thought to close mine eyes some half an hour

Boyet to Princess of France, Love's Labour's Lost **V, ii** •469

[So far from sounding and discovery]
…As is the bud bit with an envious worm
Ere he can spread his sweet leaves to the air

Montague, to Benvolio of Romeo's private melancholy, Romeo and Juliet, I, i •470

I pray you, mar no more trees with writing love-songs in their barks

Jacques to Orlando, As You Like It, III, ii •471

The third day comes a frost, a killing frost

Cardinal Wolsey, on the state of man, King Henry VIII, III, ii •472

185

Sap cheque'd with frost and lusty leaves quite gone,
Beauty o'ersnowed and bareness everywhere

Sonnet V •473

Flowers are like the pleasure of the world

Imogen (on seeing Cloten's body – not so cheery really!), Cymbeline, IV, ii •474

The rose looks fair, but fairer we it deem
For that sweet odour which doth in it live

Sonnet 54 •475

How chance the roses there do fade so fast?

Lysander to Hermia, of her blushing cheek, A Midsummer Night's Dream, I, i •476

[I'll say she looks as clear]
As morning roses newly washed with dew

Petruchio, on his plan to win Katherina, Taming of the Shrew, II, i •477

Hoary-headed frosts
Fall in the fresh lap of the crimson rose

Titania to Oberon, A Midsummer Night's Dream, II, i •478

I know a bank whereon the wild thyme blows,
Where oxslips and the nodding violet grows,
Quite over-canopied with luscious woodbine,
With sweet musk-roses, and with eglantine

Oberon, A Midsummer Night's Dream, II, i •479

A violet in the youth of primy nature,
Forward, not permanent, sweet, not lasting,
The perfume and suppliance of a minute

Laertes to Ophelia, of Hamlet's favour, Hamlet, **I, iii** •480

When daffodils begin to peer,
With the heigh! the doxy over the dale,
Why, then comes in the sweet o' the year;
For the red blood reigns in the winter's pale

Autolycus (singing), The Winter's Tale, **IV, iii** •481

O mickle is the powerful grace that lies
In herbs, plants, stones, and their true qualities:
For nought so vile that on the earth doth live
But to the earth some special good doth give

Friar Laurence, soliloquizing, Romeo and Juliet **II, iii** •482

Camomile, the more it is trodden the faster it grows

Falstaff to Prince Henry, Henry VI, **Part I, Act II, vi** •483

Such wither'd herbs as these Are meet for plucking up

Titus, Titus Andronicus, III, i •484

Lilies that fester smell far worse than weeds.
Sonnet 94 •485

Daffodils That come before the swallow dares, and take The winds of March with beauty

Perdita to Camillo and others, The Winter's Tale IV, iv •486

There's rosemary, that's for remembrance…
and there is pansies, that's for thoughts

Ophelia, distributing flowers in her madness, Hamlet, IV, v •487

Yet mark'd I where the bolt of Cupid fell:
It fell upon a little western flower,
Before milk-white, now purple, with love's wound,
And maidens call it love-in-idleness.

Oberon, on the love-inducing flower,
A Midsummer Night's Dream II, i •488

Honeysuckles, ripen'd by the sun,
Forbid the sun to enter

Hero to Margaret, Much Ado About Nothing III, i •489

The marigold, that goes to bed wi' the sun
And rises with him weeping

Perdita to Camillo and others, The Winter's Tale IV, iv •490

The fairest flowers o' the season
Are our carnations and streak'd gillyvors

Perdita to Camillo and others, The Winter's Tale IV, iv •491

Pale primroses
That die unmarried, ere they can behold
Bright Phoebus in his strength

Perdita to Camillo, A Winter's Tale, **IV, iv** •492

To paint the lily,
To throw a perfume on the violet
… Is wasteful and ridiculous excess

Salisbury to the King, King John, **IV, ii** •493

When daisies pied and violets blue
And lady-smocks all silver-white
And cuckoo-buds of yellow hue
Do paint the meadows with delight

The Song of Spring, Love's Labour's Lost, **V, ii** •494

Small herbs have grace, great weeds do grow apace

York quoting his uncle, Gloucester, Richard III, **II, iv** •495

Out of this nettle, danger, we pluck this flower, safety

Hotspur, Henry IV Part I, **II,iii** •496

Summer's lease hath all too short a date

Sonnet XVIII •497

Let the garden door be shut, and leave me to my hearing.

Olivia, requesting privacy to hear Viola, Twelfth Night, III, i •498

All gardens, even the most native and naturalistic, benefit from the hand of an artful pruner. In this season, where the garden is poised for the green flood of springtime, remember that our gardens are co-creations, shared with mother earth. And like any good mother, she expects you to tidy up your room. Now get clipping!

Tom Spencer, Soul of the Garden •499

Good gardening and a quiet life seldom go hand in hand.

Christopher Lloyd, In My Garden •500

There's little risk of becoming overly proud of one's garden
because gardening by its very nature is humbling.
It has a way of keeping you on your knees.

Joanne R. Barwick, in Readers Digest •501

Our England is a garden, and such gardens are not made by singing, 'oh, how beautiful,' and sitting in the shade.

Rudyard Kipling, **The Glory of the Garden** •502

How stuffy of Kipling. How priggish, and anyway, why not? Surely ruminating and lolling, squandering slivers of time as you ponder on this or that plan; perching about the place on seats chosen for their essential and individual quality, are other whole aspects of being a gardener. Why shouldn't we? We sit in other people's gardens, why not in our own?

Mirabel Osler •503

A fallow field is a sin.

John Steinbeck, **The Grapes of Wrath** •504

To lock horns with Nature, the only equipment you really need is the constitution of Paul Bunyan and the basic training of a commando.

S.J. Perelman, **Acres and Pains** •505

If gardeners had been developing from the beginning of the world by natural selection they would have evolved most probably into some kind of invertebrate.

Karel Capek, **The Gardener's Year** •506

One of the most pleasing sounds of Springtime, to be heard all over the country, is the contented cooing of osteopaths as Man picks up his garden spade. *Oliver Pritchett* •507

Most people who possess anything like an acre, or half of it, contribute weekly to the support of a gentleman known as Jobbing Gardener. You are warned of the danger that he may prove to be Garden Pest number one.

C.E. Lucas-Phillips, A New Small Garden •508

Most operations may be performed with common gloves. Thus, no gardener need have hands like bear's paws. *J.C. Loudon* •509

If gardening were easy, even under favourable circumstances, we should none of us care to do it.

Mrs C.W.Earle •510

There is a dangerous doctrine — dangerous because it precludes endless gardening pleasures — that every plant in the garden should be disease-free, bug-free, hardy to cold, resistant to heat and drought, cheap to buy and available at any garden centre. *Henry Mitchell,* **On Gardening** •511

To dig in one's own earth, with one's own spade, does life hold anything better?

Beverly Nichols •512

What will I do when I can no longer dig?

Knut Hamson, **Growth of the Soil** •513

Digging potatoes is always an adventure, somewhat akin to fishing. There is forever the possibility that the next cast — or the next thrust of the digging fork — will turn up a clunker.

Jerome Belanger •514

200

One of the things I enjoy about digging
(and there are lots of things I enjoy about it)
is the smell of the earth that is released by
the spade cutting in and lifting clods that
have been buried for a year. Not only does
the soil itself have a real scent, but the roots
of the crop or plant — even weed — that has
been growing there will also contribute to
the mix, creating something new out of the
vague remnants of last season's garden.

Montagu Don, The Sensuous Garden •515

Gardening is about enjoying the
smell of things growing in the soil,
getting dirty without feeling guilty,
and generally taking the time to
soak up a little peace and serenity.

Lindley Karstens •516

The soil is rather like a bran-tub – you get out of it what you put in.

RHS Encylopedia of Gardening •517

Contact with the brown earth cures all diseases. *Shirley Hibberd* •518

[soil] is far from dead in the sense of having returned to the inorganic world. It is still organic matter, in the transition stage between one form of life and another.

Lady Eve Belfour, **The Living Soil** •519

The fairest thing in nature, a flower,
still has its roots in earth and manure.

D H Lawrence •520

I personally like manure. I never feel
so affluent as when bringing back the
occasional load of high-class dung.

William Longgood •521

No poet I've ever heard of has written an ode to a load of
manure. Somebody should, and I'm not trying to be funny.

Ruth Stout, **The Ruth Stout No-Work Garden Book,** *1971* •522

One thing that unites all gardeners as
they contemplate the compost heap is a
belief in reincarnation, at least for plants.

Geoffrey B. Charlesworth, **The Opinionated Gardener** •523

The longer I live, the greater is my respect for manure in all its forms.

Elizabeth Von Arnim •524

Gardeners, like infants, are proud of their waste products.

Hugh Popham, Gentleman Peasants: A Gardener's ABC •525

The best fertilizer for a piece of land is the footprints of its owner.

Lyndon B. Johnson •526

The massacre of dandelions is a peculiarly satisfying occupation, a harmless and comforting outlet for the destructive element in our natures.

Clare Leighton, **For Hedges** •527

Love of flowers and vegetables is not enough to make a good gardener. He must also hate weeds. *Eugene P. Bertin* •528

Many gardeners will agree that hand-weeding is not the terrible drudgery that it is often made out to be. Some people find in it a kind of soothing monotony. It leaves their minds free to develop the plot for their next novel or to perfect a brilliant repartee with which they should have encountered a relative's latest example of unreasonableness.

Christopher Lloyd, **The Well-Tempered Garden** •529

The philosopher who said that
work well done never needs doing
over never weeded a garden.
Ray D. Everson •530

I always thought a yard was three feet, then I started mowing the lawn.
C.E. Cowman •531

Nature does not hesitate to interfere with me.
So I do not hesitate to tamper with *it*.
Henry Mitchell, One Man's Garden •532

I am fonder of my garden
for the trouble it gives me.

Reginald Farrer, My Rock-Garden •533

Genesis got it just wrong. Adam should have been exiled from town as a punishment, and put to slave in a garden.

Clarence Day, from After All, *published 1936, the year after his death* •534

My garden will never make me famous,
I'm a horticultural ignoramus.
Ogden Nash •535

My heart is a garden tired with autumn,
Heaped with bending asters and dahlias heavy and dark,
In the hazy sunshine, the garden remembers April,
The drench of rains and a snow-drop quick and clear as a spark;
Daffodils blowing in the cold wind of morning,
And golden tulips, goblets holding the rain.

The garden will be hushed with snow, forgotten soon, forgotten;
After the stillness, will spring come again?

Sara Teasdale, **The Garden** •536

Weeds are not supposed to grow,
But by degrees
Some achieve a flower, although
No one sees.

Philip Larkin, **Modesties** •537

Belbroughton Road is bonny, and pinkly bursts the spray
Of prunus and forsythia across the public way,
For the full-spring tide of blossom sethed and parted hence,
Leaving land-locked pools of jonquils by sunny garden fence.

John Betjeman, May-Day Song for North Oxford •538

this is the garden: colors come and go,
frail azures fluttering from night's outer wing
strong silent greens serenely lingering,
absolute lights like baths of golden snow.

e e cummings, this is the garden: colors come and go, ix •539

The kiss of the sun for pardon,
The song of the birds for mirth,
One is nearer God's heart in a garden
Than anywhere else on earth.

Dorothy Frances Gurney, God's Garden, *1913* •540

211

April is the cruellest month, breeding
Lilacs out of the dead land, mixing
Memory and desire, stirring,
Dull roots with spring rain.

T. S. Eliot, from The Wasteland •541

What though his phlox and hollyhocks ere half a month demised?
What though his ampelopsis clambered not as advertised?
Though every seed was guaranteed and every standard true-
Forget, forgive they did not live! Believe, and buy anew!

Rudyard Kipling, Pan in Vermont •542

The gardener searches earth and sky
The truth in nature to espy
In vain

He well might find that eager balm
In lilies' stately-statued calm;
But then

He well might find it in this fret
Of lilies rusted, rotting, wet
With rain.

Wallace Stevens,
A Room on a Garden •543

What is all this juice and all this joy?
A strain of earth's sweet being in the beginning
In Eden garden.

Gerard Manley Hopkins, Spring, *1918* •544

213

Rose, rose and clematis,
Trail and twine and clasp and kiss.

Alfred Lord Tennyson, The Window, or the Song of the Wrens •545

Come into the garden, Maud,
For the black bat, night, has flown,
Come into the garden, Maud,
I am here at the gate alone.

Alfred Lord Tennyson, Maud Winter is cold-hearted •546

Spring is yea and nay,
Autumn is a weather-cock,
Blown every way.
Summer days for me.
When every leaf is on its tree.

Christina Rossetti, Summer •547

214

In the other gardens
And all up the vale,
From the autumn bonfires
See the smoke trail!

Robert Louis Stevenson, Autumn Fires •548

I saw the next door garden lie,
Adorned with flowers before my eye,
And many pleasant places more
That I had never seen before.

Robert Louis Stevenson, Foreign Lands •549

One morning, very early, before the sun was up,
I rose and found the shining dew on every buttercup;
But my lazy little shadow, like an arrant sleepy head,
Had stayed at home behind me and was fast asleep in bed.

Robert Louis Stevenson, My Shadow, in A Children's Garden of Verses •550

Go, little book, and wish to all
Flowers in the garden, meat in the hall,
A bin of wine, a spice of wit,
A house with lawns enclosing it.

Robert Louis Stevenson, Underwoods — Envoy, *1887* •551

Behold this compost! behold it well!
What chemistry!
Earth grows such sweet things out of such corruptions.

Walt Whitman, **This Compost,** *1867* •552

Here is a brighter garden,
Where not a frost has been;
In its unfading flowers
I hear the bright bee hum;
Prithee, my brother,
Into my garden come!

Emily Dickinson, 1851 •553

Every clod feels a stir of might,
An instinct within it that reaches and towers
And groping blindly above it for light
Comes to a soul in grass and flowers.

> *James Russell Lowell,*
> The Vision of Sir Launfal, *1845* •554

The damask rose and myrtle flowers,
Narcissus and sweet pea,
With lustre shine in garden bowers,
As stars shine on the sea.

> *Thomas P. Moses* •555

Pluck not the wayside flower;
It is the traveller's dower.

> *William Allingham,* Wayside Flowers •556

There is a garden in her face, where roses and white lilies grow.

> *Thomas Campion,* Fourth Book of Airs •557

To me the meanest flower that blows can give
Thoughts that do often lie too deep for tears.

William Wordsworth, **Ode – Intimations of Immortality,** *1807* •558

A violet by the mossy stone
Half hidden from the eye!
Fair as a star when only one
Is shining in the sky.

William Wordsworth, **She Dwelt Among the Untrodden Ways** •559

In this sequestered nook how sweet
To sit upon my orchard-seat!

William Wordsworth, **The Green Linnet** •560

I wandered lonely as a cloud
That floats on high o'er vales and hills,
When all at once I saw a crowd,
A host, of golden daffodils.

William Wordsworth, I Wandered Lonely as a Cloud, *1804* •561

'Tis my faith that every flower Enjoys the air it breathes!

William Wordsworth, Lines Written in Early Spring, pub. *1798* •562

Spade! Thou art a tool of honor in my hands.
I press thee, through a yielding soil, with pride.

William Wordsworth,
To The Spade of A Friend •563

Shed no tear! O, shed no tear!
The flower will bloom another year.
Weep no more! O, weep no more!
Young buds sleep in the root's white core.

John Keats, **Fairy Song** •564

The poetry of the earth is never dead.

John Keats, **The Grasshopper and the Cricket** •565

The Sensitive Plant was the earliest
Up-gathered into the bosom of the rest;
A sweet child weary of its delight
The feeblest and yet the favourite.

Percy Bysshe Shelley, The Sensitive Plant, Part I •566

Who loves a garden loves a greenhouse too.

William Cowper, The Task, Book III: The Garden *1785* •567

The bud may have a bitter taste,
But sweet will be the flower.

William Cowper, Light Shining Out of Darkness, from Olney Hymns •568

To create a little flower is the labour of ages.

William Blake, The Marriage of Heaven and Hell, *1793* •569

Take thy plastic spade,
It is thy pencil; take thy seeds, thy plants,
They are thy colours.

William Mason, **The English Garden,** *1782* •570

A scene beyond Elysium blest;
Where sculptur'd elegance and native grace,
Unite to stamp the beauties of the place;
While sweetly blending, still one seen,
The wavy lawn, the sloping green;
While novelty, with cautious cunning,
Through ev'ry maze of fancy running,
From China borrows aids to deck the scene...

Oliver Goldsmith on Kew, **Threnodia Augustalia,** *1772* •571

Beauteous the garden's umbrage mild,
Walk, water, meditated wild,
And all the gloomy beds.

Christopher Smart, A Song to David *c1763*, written while
Smart was confined to an asylum •572

Ye beauties! O how great the sum
Of sweetness that ye bring;
On what charity ye come
To bless the latter spring!
How kind the visit that ye pay,
Like strangers on a rainy day.

Christopher Smart, On A Bed of Guernsey Lilies, *1764* •573

I have a garden of my own
But so with roses overgrown,
And lillies, that you would it guess
To be a little wilderness.

Andrew Marvell, **The Nymph Complaining**
for the Death of Her Fawn, *1681* •574

Make that the tulips may have share
Of sweetness, seeing they are fair,
And roses of their thorns disarm;
But most procure
That violets may a longer age endure.

Andrew Marvell, **The Picture of**
Little T.C. in a Prospect of Flowers •575

How could such sweet and wholesome hours
Be reckoned but with herbs and flowers.

Andrew Marvell, **The Garden,** *1681* •576

Annihilating all that is made
to a green thought in a green shade.

Andrew Marvell, **The Garden,** *1681* •577

Here at the fountain's sliding foot,
Or at some fruit tree's mossy root,
Casting the body's vest aside,
My soul into the boughs does glide.

Andrew Marvell, The Garden, *1681* •578

Fair Quiet, have I found thee here, And Innocence thy sister dear?

Andrew Marvell, The Garden, *1681* •579

The Gods, that mortal beauty chase,
Still in a tree did end their race;
Apollo hunted Daphne so
Only that she might laurel grow.

Andrew Marvell, The Garden, *1681* •580

Get up, sweet Slug-a-bed, and see
The dew bespangling herb and tree.

Robert Herrick, **Corinna's Going a-Maying,** *1648* •581

Fair daffodils, we weep to see
You haste away so soon:
As yet the early-rising sun
Has not attained his noon.

Robert Herrick, **To Daffodils,** *1648* •582

Gather ye rosebuds while ye may,
Old Time is still a-flying:
And this same flower that smiles to-day,
To-morrow will be dying.

Robert Herrick, **To the Virgins,**
to Make Much of Time, *1648* •583

226

And add to these retired Leisure
That in trim gardens takes his pleasure.

John Milton, Il Penseroso', *1645* •584

...the crisped brooks
Ran nectar, visiting each plant, and fed
Flowers worthy of Paradise which not nice art
In beds and curious knots, but Nature boon
Poured forth profuse on hill, and dale, and plains.

John Milton, Paradise Lost, Book IV •585

Each beauteous flower,
Iris all hues, Roses, and Gessamin
Rear'd high thir flourisht heads between, and wrought
Mosaic; underfoot the Violet,
Crocus, and Hyacinth with rich inlay
Broider'd the ground, more coloured than with stone
Of costliest Emblem. *John Milton,* Paradise Lost, IV, *1667* •586

Let us divide our labours, thou where choice
Leads thee, or where most needs whether to wind
The Woodbine round this Arbor, or direct
The clasping ivy where it climb, while I
In yonder Spring of Roses intermixt
With Myrtle, find what to redress till Noon.

John Milton, Paradise Lost, IX, *1667* •587

227

There the most daintie paradise on the ground
It selfe doth offer to his sober eye,
In which all pleasures plenteously abownd,
And none does others happinesse envye:

Edmund Spenser, The Faerie Queene,
Book II in the Bower of Bliss •588

In that same Gardin all the goodly flowres,
Wherewith dame Nature doth her beautifie,
And decks the girlonds of her paramoures,
Are fetcht.

Edmund Spenser, The Faerie Queene,
Book III - in the Garden of Adonis •589

In March and in Aprill, from morning to night:
In sowing and setting, good huswives delight;
To have in a garden, or other like plot:
To trim up their house, and to furnish the pot.

Thomas Tusser, Hundredth Good Pointes of Husbandrie, *1557* •590

228

…Of al the floures in the mede,
Thanne love I most thise floures white and rede,
Swiche as men callen dayses in our toun…
Allas, that I ne had Englyssh, ryme or prose,
Suffisant this flour to preyse aryght!

Geoffrey Chaucer, Prologue to
The Legend of Good Women, *c.1380-87* •591

Ful gay was al the ground, and quaint,
And powdred, as men had it peint,
With many a fressh and sundry flower,
That casten up ful good savour.

Geoffrey Chaucer, **the Romaunt of the Rose** •592

A garden inclosed is my sister, my spouse,
a spring shut up, a fountain sealed.

Bible (King James Version), **Song of Solomon 4:12** •593

229

The flower appears on the earth; the time of the singing of the birds is come, and the voice of the turtle is heard in our land. *Bible (King James Version)*
Song of Solomon 2:12 •594

230

A friend of mine, whose own fingers are of the greenest, reproaches me from time to time for making gardening sound too easy. My optimism, she says, is misleading.

Vita Sackville West, **In Your Garden Again** •595

– I very earnestly wish I may
die before you, Mr Brown.
– Why so?
– Because I should like to see Heaven
before you have improved it.

Conversation reported to have taken place between
eighteenth century landscape gardener Lancelot
'Capability Brown' and a contemporary, (quoted by
Jenny Uglow in A Little History of British Gardening*)* •596

The delicate droop of petals
standing out in relief is like
the eyelid of a child.

Auguste Rodin •597

232

I perhaps owe having become a painter to flowers. *Claude Monet* •598

Gertrude Jekyll, like Monet, was a painter with poor eyesight, and their gardens — his at Giverny in the Seine valley, hers in Surrey — had resemblances that may have sprung from this condition. Both loved plants that foamed and frothed over walls and pergolas, spread in tides beneath trees; both saw flowers in islands of colored light – an image the normal eye captures only by squinting.

Eleanor Perenyi, Green Thoughts •599

There is nothing more difficult for a truly creative painter than to paint a rose, because before he can do so he has first to forget all the roses that were ever painted. *Henri Matisse* •600

Art is the unceasing effort to compete with the beauty of flowers and never succeeding.

Marc Chagall •601

When you take a flower in your hand and really look at it, it's your world for the moment. I want to give that world to someone else. Most people in the city rush around so, they have no time to look at a flower.

Georgia O'Keeffe, **New York Post** •602

I hate flowers; I paint them because they're cheaper than models and they don't move.

Georgia O'Keeffe •603

234

All gardens are a form of autobiography.

Robert Dash, artist •604

Paradise haunts gardens, and some gardens are paradises.
Mine is one of them. Others are like bad children —
spoilt by their parents, over-watered and covered with
noxious chemicals. *Derek Jarman* •605

In the spring, at the end of the day, you should smell like dirt.

Margaret Atwood •606

I'm not really a career person. I'm a gardener, basically.

George Harrison •607

If I were to choose where to die, it would be in the herbaceous border.

Miriam Stoppard •608

Come on! How often do you prune your eugenia myrtifolia right after it blooms, the way Martha Stewart does, in December, wearing your lipstick?

Anne Raver, Deep in the Green •609

Gardening is a humbling experience.

Martha Stewart, no stranger to humbling experiences in recent years •610

When at last I took time to look into the heart of a flower, it opened up a whole new world – a world where every country walk would be an adventure, where every garden would become an enchanted one... as if a window had been opened to let in the sun.

Princess Grace of Monaco •611

I try to express in a physical form what I feel on an inner level. I think a garden should delight the eye, warm the heart and feed the soul. *HRH Prince Charles* •612

To get the best results, you must talk to your vegetables.

HRH Prince Charles •613

I just come and talk to the plants, really — very important to talk to them, they respond I find.

HRH Prince Charles, 1986, Television interview •614

You've given a lot of ladies a lot of pleasure.

Her Majesty The Queen, presenting Alan Titchmarsh with his MBE (apocryphal) •615

The art of gardening. In this the artist who lays out the work, and devises a garment for a piece of ground, has the delight of seeing his work live and grow hour by hour; and, while it is growing, he is able to polish, to cut and carve, to fill up here and there, to hope, and to love.

Prince Albert, Queen Victoria's consort •616

A traveller should be
a botanist, for in all
views plants form the
chief embellishment.

Charles Darwin •617

Flowers are restful
to look at. They have
neither emotions
nor conflicts.

Sigmund Freud •618

The Nation that destroys its soil destroys itself.

Franklin D. Roosevelt, **Letter to all State Governors on a Uniform Soil Conservation Law (February 26, 1937)** •619

Die when I may, I want it said of me by those who know me best, that I always plucked a thistle and planted a flower where I thought a flower would grow.

Abraham Lincoln •620

But though an old man, I am but a young gardener.

Thomas Jefferson, **letter of 1811** •621

What nature has done for us is sublime and beautiful and unique.

Thomas Jefferson, **letter of 1811** •622

You can lead a horticulture, but you can't make her think.

Dorothy Parker, legendary wit. This, allegedly, was Parker's response to a challenge to compose an epigram containing the word horticulture •623

The flowers out there smell like dirty old dollar bills.

Dorothy Parker on Hollywood •624

My main ambition as a gardener is to water my orange trees with gin, then all I have to do is squeeze the juice into a glass. *W. C. Fields* •625

Don't think I haven't tried; I have fertilized my crops with a variety of stimulants. I have scattered Hitler's speeches and most of DuPont's most expensive chemicals over their stunted growths, but so far all I have to show for my trouble is a small bed of wild marijuana, a sprig of mint, and a dislocation of the trunk muscles that has an excellent chance of developing into a full-blown rupture... I only hope that Uncle Sam isn't relying too heavily on my Victory Crop to sustain the nation through the coming winter.

Groucho Marx, Groucho Marx and Other Short Stories and Tall Tales, 1993, *ed. Robert S. Bader* •626

I appreciate the misunderstanding I have had with Nature over my perennial border. I think it is a flower garden; she thinks it is a meadow lacking grass, and tries to correct the error.

S.J. Perelman, Acres and Pains •627

As the poet said, 'Only God can make a tree', probably because it's so hard to figure out how to get the bark on.

Woody Allen •628

Of all the wonders of nature, a tree in summer is perhaps the most remarkable; with the possible exception of a moose singing *Embraceable You* in spats.

Woody Allen •629

My neighbour asked if he could borrow my lawnmower and I told him of course so long as he didn't take it out of my garden.

Eric Morecambe •630

Even more dreadful than the dreadful passer-by is the London dog. The combination of a dog and owner is a law unto itself, as I realised when I watched a dog-owner hold open my gate so that her deformed pooch could direct his streaming ammoniac jet into the smiling faces of my auriculas.

Germaine Greer •631

Millions of women between the ages of forty-five and fifty-five discover gardening. Other people imagine that this is because they have nothing else to do. In fact there is always something else to do, as every woman who gardens knows.

Germaine Greer •632

Britain in Bloom goes around this country spreading flowers like a disease.

Roy Strong, writer, critic, snob. •633

244

The only Zen you'll find
flowering in the garden
is the Zen you bring
there each day.

Michael P. Garofalo •634

The soul cannot thrive in the absence of a garden. If you don't want paradise, you are not human; and if you are not human you don't have a soul.

Thomas Moore, The Reenchantment of Everyday Life •635

The sun, with all those plants revolving around it and dependent upon it, can still ripen a bunch of grapes as if it had nothing else in the universe to do.

Galileo •636

There can be no other occupation like gardening
in which, if you were to creep up on someone at
their work, you would find them smiling.

Mirabel Osler •637

There is no other door to knowledge than the door
Nature opens; and there is no truth except the
truths we discover in Nature. *Luther Burbank* •638

This soil of ours, this precious heritage,
what an unobtrusive existence it leads!...
To the rich soil let us give the credit due.
The soil is the reservoir of life.

J.A. Toogood, **Our Soil and Water** •639

Touch the earth, love the earth, honour
the earth, her plains, her valleys, her hills, and
her seas; rest your spirit in her solitary places.

Henry Beston, **The Outermost House** •640

We have descended into the garden and caught three hundred slugs. How I love the mixture of the beautiful and the squalid in gardening. It makes it so lifelike.

Evelyn Underhill, Letters •641

As long as one has a garden one has a future; and as long as one has a future one is alive.

Frances Hodgson Burnett, In the Garden •642

We learn from our gardens to deal with the most urgent question of the time: How much is enough?

Wendell Berry •643

Better to eat vegetables and fear no creditors, than eat duck and hide from them. *The Talmud* •644

Gardeners, I think, dream bigger dreams than emperors.
Mary Cantwell •645

Show me your garden and I shall tell you what you are.

Alfred Austin •646

Gardens are places in which to fantasise. You can legitimately be Lord or Lady Muck for a while, and sometimes even dress up for the occasion. Try on straw hats in secret before going out in them, however; they can look very silly.

Josephine Saxton, **Gardening Down a Rabbit Hole** •647

Heaven is under our feet as well as over our heads.

Henry David Thoreau •648

I continue to handpick the beetles, mosquitoes feast on me, birds eat the mosquitoes, something else eats the birds, and so on up and down the biotic pyramid. *William Longgood* •649

I like trees because they seem more resigned to the way they have to live than other things do. I feel as if this tree knows everything I ever think of when I sit here. When I come back to it, I never have to remind it of anything; I begin just where I left off. *Willa Cather,* O Pioneers! •650

I think that if ever a mortal heard the voice of God it would be in a garden at the cool of the day.
F. Frankfort Moore, A Garden of Peace •651

If Bibles fail, each garden will descry the works of God to us.
William Prynne, pamphleteer, quoted in **A Little History of British Gardening** •652

It is only when you start to plant a garden
– probably after fifty – that you realise that
something important happens every day.

Geoffrey B. Charlesworth, The Opinionated Gardener •653

Oak trees come out of acorns,
no matter how unlikely that
seems. An acorn is just a tree's
way back into the ground. For
another try. Another trip
through. One life for another.

Shirley Ann Grau, American novelist and short story writer •654

Our Cottage-Gardening Society… has reclaimed
many a waste place from sterility, many a sot from the
beerhouse, and brought comfort to many a house.

Samuel Reynolds Hole, on the positive effects of 'missionary floristry',
writing in the 1880s •655

Seedsmen reckon that their stock in trade is not seeds at all… it's optimism. *Geoff Hamilton* •656

Gardening's such an optimistic activity. By sowing a seed you're investing in the future. And gardening, unlike life, gives us all endless second chances.

Gay Search •657

Soil is a resource, a living, breathing entity that, if treated properly, will maintain itself. It's our lifeline for survival. When it has finally been depleted, the human population will disappear.

Marjorie Harris •658

The gardener must be a philosopher, accepting that he and his have a place in the cycle of life which nothing, or very little, can alter.

Hugh Johnson, Hugh Johnson's Gardening Companion •659

The joy of the Husbandman is not a flash and so away, but it is a settled and habituall joy…which also keeps the spirits cheerful and lively: for there are many renovations, and a continual progress to the more benigne, and things mending and growing to the better.

Ralph Austen, The Spiritual Use of an Orchard'
in his Treatise on Fruit Trees, *1653* •660

If seeds in the black earth can turn into such beautiful roses, what might not the heart of man become in its long journey toward the stars?

G.K. Chesterton •661

Let me define a garden as the meeting of raw nature and the human imagination in which both seek the fulfilment of their beauty.

Thomas Moore, The Reenchantment of Everyday Life •662

That we find a crystal or a poppy beautiful means that we are less alone, that we are more deeply inserted into existence than the course of a single life would lead us to believe.

John Berger, The Sense of Sight •663

You do not need to know anything about a plant to know that it is beautiful.

Montagu Don, The Sensuous Garden •664

There is no such thing as an ugly garden — gardens, like babies, are beautiful to their parents.

Ken Druse, The Collector's Garden •665

Planting ground is painting the landscape with living things.

Gertrude Jekyll •666

When the eye is trained to perceive pictorial effect, it is frequently struck by something – some combination of grouping, lighting and colour — that is seen to have that complete aspect of unity and beauty that to the artist's eye forms a picture. Such are the impressions that the artist-gardener endeavours to produce in every portion of the garden.

Gertrude Jekyll •667

Garden making is a creative work…It is a personal expression of self, an individual conception of beauty.

Hanna Rion, Let's Make a Flower Garden •668

One thing is certain, and the rest is lies;
The flower that once hath blown for ever dies.

The Rubáiyát of Omar Khayyám, *1859* •669

One of the attractive things about flowers is their beautiful reserve.

Henry David Thoreau •670

256

Flowers are beautiful hieroglyphics
of nature, with which she indicates
how much she loves us. *Goethe* •671

Correct handling of flowers refines the personality.
Gustie L. Herrigel, **Zen in the Art of Flower Arrangement** •672

All the flowers of all the tomorrows are in the seeds of today.
Indian proverb •673

Bread feeds the body, indeed,
but flowers feed also the soul.
The Koran •674

Earth laughs in flowers.

Ralph Waldo Emerson, Hamatreya •675

Science, or para-science, tells us that geraniums bloom better if they are spoken to. But a kind word every now and then is really quite enough. Too much attention, like too much feeding, and weeding and hoeing, inhibits and embarrasses them.

Victoria Glendinning •676

When we learn to call flowers by name we take the first step toward a real intimacy with them.

Mrs. William Starr Dana •677

We may think we are tending our garden,
but of course, in many different ways, it is the
garden and the plants that are nurturing us.

Jenny Uglow, **A Little History of British Gardening** •678

Now I see the secret of making
the best persons. It is to grow
in the open air, and to eat and
sleep with the earth.

Walt Whitman, Leaves of Grass •679

Like the fruits, when cooler weather and frosts arrive, we too are
braced and ripened. When we shift from the shady to the sunny side
of the house, and sit there in an extra coat for warmth, our green and
leafy and pulpy thoughts acquire colour and flavour, and perchance
a sweet nuttiness at last, worth your cracking. *Henry David Thoreau* •680

He who sows the ground with care and diligence
acquires a greater stock of religious merit than he
could gain by the repetition of ten thousand prayers.

Zoroaster •681

259

Green fingers are the extension
of a verdant heart. *Russell Page* •682

Gardening is not a rational act.

Margaret Atwood, **Bluebeard's Egg** •683

Gardening is a long road, with many detours and way stations,
and here we all are at one point or another. It's not a question
of superior or inferior taste, merely a question of which detour
we are on at the moment. Getting there (as they say) is not
important; the wandering about in the wilderness or
in the olive groves or in the bayous is the whole point.

Henry Mitchell, **Gardening is a Long Road** •684

Gardening requires lots
of water — most of it in
the form of perspiration.

Lou Erickson •685

A woman is like a tree. You must judge it not by its flowers, but by its fruit.

Sarel Bok as Xhabbo in A Far Off Place •686

Gardening is civil and social, but it wants the vigour and freedom of the forest and the outlaw.
Henry David Thoreau •687

Gardens always mean something else, man absolutely uses one thing to say another.

Robert Harbison, **Eccentric Spaces** •688

Our gardens are symbols of home rather than seduction. Young people with fire in their blood are seldom found in them. The garden is the scene of middle age, of the slow passage from sexual excitement to domestic routine.
Robert Scruton, **Financial Times** •689

Planting can foster a sense of belonging.

Jenny Uglow, **A Little History of British Gardening** •690

Plants don't point a finger. If they live, they don't carry grudges. If they die, unless you've killed an entire species or a rain forest, you feel only a momentary guilt, which is quickly replaced by a philosophical, smug feeling: Failure is enriching your compost pile.

Anne Raver, **Deep in the Green** •691

The great challenge for the garden designer is not to make the garden look natural, but to make the garden so that the people in it will feel natural.

Lawrence Halprin, **American landscape architect** •692

The true meaning of life is to plant trees, under whose shade you do not expect to sit.
Nelson Henderson, quoted in 'Songs of Joy' by Joan D. Chittister •693

To create a garden is to search for a better world ….. hope for the future is at the heart of all gardening.

Marina Schinz •694

Unemployment is capitalism's way of getting you to plant a garden.

Orson Scott Card •695

Vegetable gardening might be considered one of the great conservative rituals.

David M Tucker •696

Gardens, scholars say, are the first sign of commitment to a community. When people plant corn they are saying, let's stay here. And by their connection to the land, they are connected to one another.

Anne Raver, **Deep in the Green** •697

A garden is a symbol of man's arrogance, perverting nature to human ends...

Tim Smit •698

Exclusiveness in a garden is a mistake as great as it is in society.

Alfred Austin •699

Pessimistic moods, like caterpillars, feed on the gardener's happiness.

Deborah Kellaway, **The Making of an English Country Garden** •700

A lawn is nature under totalitarian rule.

Michael Pollan, **Second Nature** •701

264

Gardening is…an outlet for fanaticism, violence,
love, and rationality without their worst side effects.

Geoffrey B. Charlesworth, **A Gardener Obsessed** •702

Of all human activities, apart from the procreation of
children, gardening is the most optimistic and hopeful.
The gardener is by definition one who plans for and believes
and trusts in a future, whether in the short or long term.

Susan Hill, **Through the Garden Gate** •703

The more I hear of Horticulture,
the more I like plain gardening.

Julian R. Meade, **Bouquets & Bitters** •704

The act of pollination is the foundation
upon which civilisation stands.

Marian Williams, **Arboretum Leaves** •705

Those that are wasters and willful spoilers of trees and plants,
without just reason to do so, have seldom prospered in this world.

Moses Cook •706

To forget how to dig the earth and to tend the soil is to forget ourselves. *Mahatma Gandhi* •707

It's great to see gardening being hailed as the new rock 'n' roll… Gardening is a vast and untapped reservoir of inspiration. So lock up your garden tools — the new rock and roll is here.

Kim Wilde, **Wilde About Gardening** *column in* **Prima** *magazine* •708

Our new modern gardens are... just beginning to reflect the rich, mixed cultures of our society.

Jenny Uglow, A Little History of British Gardening, *on the influx of tropical species in modern gardening* •709

Garden... start with big months of sweat and toil, big ideas and aching joints, excitements and disappointments, successes and failures, laughter and tears. Until one fine day you realise that you're hooked and your home plot has become a part of you that you simply can't let go.

Geoff Hamilton •710

There is nothing like a garden for making you feel small. There you are, right in the middle of the greatest miracle of all – the world of growing things. *Geoff Hamilton* •711

Kew is more than just a garden. It is both an historical tableau and the cutting edge of scientific research. It is 35 years since I first set foot in the place, but it still holds a unique place in my affections.
Alan Titchmarsh, **a graduate of Kew Diploma Course** •712

There isn't a right or wrong. There's my way and there's your way, and as long as they grow… It's self-expression that counts. *Alan Titchmarsh,* The Guardian •713

One can never underestimate the force of a nurturing man with a trowel; if Alan Titchmarsh can get women moist, then Monty Don will unleash a whole water feature.

Simon Garfield, journalist, The Observer •714

The British have such an odd relationship with food — and the land. I want the public and the Soil Association to see that growing things in a garden is no different to growing things in a field. *Montagu Don, in* The Observer, *2009* •715

I've never been in a garden I prefer to my own.

Montagu Don, echoing the belief of many serious gardeners •716

Charlie Dimmock isn't a real person, of course. She's actually a robot created by some shadowy military-industrial-gardening organisation to encourage us to get on with horticultural shenanigans while they spray us with sedatives from weather balloons. And those aren't nipples, you know — they're control buttons.

Gareth McLean, **The Guardian** •717

It is rather ridiculous that a woman doing manual work is still seen as something to make a fuss about. It's clear from the people who come into the garden centre that it's the women who do the gardening.

Charlie Dimmock •718

None of my boyfriends has ever told me I was sexy or attractive. I think people only say that sort of thing in films.

Charlie Dimmock •719

He's copying Charlie — he doesn't wear a bra either!

Richard Madeley on Diarmuid Gavin •720

All I've ever really wanted has been the chance to explore the potential of what a garden can be.

Diarmuid Gavin, **The Observer** •721

There's an elitism in gardening. It's rare to see a non-white face at Chelsea [Flower Show]. But all that is changing.

Diarmuid Gavin, **The Observer** •722

The gardens we make are akin to some of the more outrageous outfits worn by models on catwalks. Some are there to provoke ideas, thoughts and reactions, but not necessarily to copy.

Diarmuid Gavin, presenter of **Home Front In The Garden** •723

My job is to work people into a bubbling froth of excitement over the boundless possibilities that lie outside their doors. If I do my job well, then the world will be a little more beautiful and people will be a little bit happier. What more could anybody wish from their life?

James Alexander-Sinclair •724

There's no such thing as the garden police.

James Alexander-Sinclair encourages self-expression •725

He's Britain's leading organic gardener, but he's also been a chicken giblet washer, computer installation engineer, council cleaner, dog impersonator, glass fibre laminator, houseboy and cook in a house of ill repute, security lighting engineer, marine engineer, museum attendant, nude model, official guide in Paris, theatrical gofer, vitreous enamel applicator, arcade mechanic and inventor.

Bob Flowerdew's biography on the BBC website www.bbc.co.uk •726

I like to come home and water my plants, do some weeding. I love garden centres and all those statues of naked people. I have a bunch of them.

Caprice, model •727

I have no plants in my house. They won't live for me. Some of them don't even wait to die, they commit suicide.

Jerry Seinfeld •728

She does not fret father, or if she does you well
know the cause is your indifference — a house,
a garden, a horse, a wife the preferential order.

Anne Louise Lambert as Mrs Tallmann in **The Draughtsman's Contract** •729

Lutton Gowts (n): The
opposite of green fingers,
the effortless propensity
to cause plant death.

from **The Meaning of Liff** *by Douglas Adams and John Lloyd* •730

That's what I like about plants – they don't answer back.

Helen Mirren as Georgina Woodhouse in Greenfingers •731

This is an Anglo-Dutch garden, madam, with French influence. We have progressed from flowers. A garden is a celebration of art's triumph over nature.

Ewan MacGregor as Meneer Chrome in Serpent's Kiss •732

They took all the trees, and
  put them in a tree museum,
And they charged the people a
  dollar and a half just to see 'em.
Don't it always seem to go that
  you don't know what you've
  got 'til it's gone.
They paved paradise
And put up a parking lot.

Joni Mitchell, Big Yellow Taxi •733

An Englishman's home may be his castle,
but it's the grounds that the Englishwoman
cares about. *Wendy Holden, novelist* •734

If something wants to grow somewhere, why not encourage it?
Although that sounds like mitigation for being a bad gardener
rather than a plan. I like to think of myself as a natural gardener!

Clive Anderson's laid-back approach to his garden •735

I get a lot of flack from people who say
you can't be a real gardener and try
and grow your nails. But I wear gloves
when I'm doing serious gardening, to
protect my hands from toxoplasmosis.

Rachel de Thame, former model turned celebrity gardener •736

We'll leave the last word to an old Bob Monkouse gag •737

What do old gardeners
do when they retire?

Bibliography

Brother Cadfael's Herb Garden
Whiteman /Talbot, *1996* (Little, Brown)

Complete Book of Gardening
Alan Titchmarsh, *1999* (BBC)

Flora Britannica
Richard Mabey, *1996* (Chatto & Windus)

The Gardener's Companion
2004 (Robson)

Garden Lovers Quotations
1992 (Exley)

A Gardener's Bouquet of Quotations
Maria Polushkin Robbins (Ed), *1994* (Robert Hale)

The Littlest Gardening Giftbook
2000 (Exley)

A Little History of British Gardening
Jenny Uglow, *2005* (Pimlico)

The Oxford Dictionary of Quotations
Elizabeth Knowles (Ed), *1999* (Oxford University Press)

Meetings With Remarkable Trees
Thomas Pakenham, *1996* (Weidenfeld & Nicholson)

New Flower Expert
Dr D.G.Hessayon, *1999* (Expert Books)

Organic Bible
Bob Flowerdew, *1998* (Kyle Cathie)

Painted Garden
2000 (Running Press)

The Quotable Gardener
Kathy Ishizuka (Ed), *2000* (McGraw-Hill Companies)

The Quotable Gardener
2002 (The Lyons Press)

The Royal Horticultural Society: Treasury of Garden Writing
Charles Elliot (Ed), *2005* (Frances Lincoln Publishers Ltd.)

Shakespeare Quotations
G.F. Lamb (Ed), *1994* (Larousse)

Thoreau: A Book of Quotations
2000 (Dover)